"Mark Noll invites us to join him on the intellectual and spiritual journey that led him to realize that Christianity from its origin onward must be understood and evaluated as both cross-cultural and global. Noll points out significant signposts along the way that encouraged him to reconsider the methodologies he employed as a historian of Christianity and to embrace an approach that combines serious historical scholarship with greater attention to broad and local contexts, empathetic interpretation, thoughtful criticism, and history as theology. As an 'autobiographical memoir,' this engaging book gives insight into the mind of an important scholar today, but it also summons historians and scholars in other fields to assess the approaches they take in the study of Christianity."

—**Karen Westerfield Tucker**, Boston University

"Mark Noll provides a rare glimpse into the mind and heart of a historian as he reflects on the intertwining of his own professional and personal story with the story of world Christianity. The book leaves us hungry to know more—more about how the study of history can enrich our own spiritual journeys, more about the rich and unfolding story of a changing scholarly and pedagogical orientation toward world Christianity, and more about the power of the gospel as the incarnate Word both finds itself 'at home' in and at the same time transcends the particularities of every culture of the globe. This book has the potential to kindle many productive conversations among friends and colleagues in both the church and the academy!"

—**Shirley A. Mullen**, president, Houghton College

"Mark Noll's story of how he came to engage world Christianity is powerful and instructive—and a delight to read. It should be required reading for seminarians and widely discussed in churches interested in the global contours of the Christian faith. Here we witness how thinking changed, but much more—how a life was reordered and transformed."

—**Nathan O. Hatch**, president, Wake Forest University

TURNING ◆◆
S
O
U
T
H

TURNING SOUTH:
CHRISTIAN SCHOLARS IN AN AGE
OF WORLD CHRISTIANITY

Joel Carpenter, *series editor*

The Turning South: Christian Scholars in an Age of World Christianity series offers reflections by eminent Christian scholars who have turned their attention and commitments toward the global South and East. In order to inspire and move the rising generation of Christian scholars in the Northern Hemisphere to engage the thought world and issues of the global South more vigorously, the series books highlight such reorientations and ask what the implications of "turning South" are for Christian thought and creativity in a variety of cultural fields.

Also available in the series

Journey toward Justice: Personal Encounters in the Global South
Nicholas P. Wolterstorff

*Reading a Different Story: A Christian Scholar's
Journey from America to Africa*
Susan VanZanten

TURNING
SOUTH

FROM EVERY TRIBE AND NATION

A HISTORIAN'S DISCOVERY OF THE GLOBAL CHRISTIAN STORY

MARK A. NOLL

Baker Academic

a division of Baker Publishing Group
Grand Rapids, Michigan

© 2014 by Mark A. Noll

Published by Baker Academic
a division of Baker Publishing Group
P.O. Box 6287, Grand Rapids, MI 49516-6287
www.bakeracademic.com

Printed in the United States of America

Library of Congress Cataloging-in-Publication Data
Noll, Mark A., 1946–
    From every tribe and nation : a historian's discovery of the global Christian story / Mark A. Noll.
        p.   cm. — (Turning south: Christian scholars in an age of world Christianity)
    Includes bibliographical references and index.
    ISBN 978-0-8010-3993-5 (pbk.)
        1. Noll, Mark A., 1946– 2. Church historians—United States—Biography.
    3. Church history—Study and teaching. 4. Christianity—Study and teaching.
    I. Title.
    BR139.N65A3 2014
    270.072'02—dc23   2014016679
    [B]

Some material in chapter 3 is taken from the following: "Remembering Arthur F. Holmes (1924–2011)" by Mark Noll, *EerdWord* (blog), October 17, 2011, reprinted by permission of the William B. Eerdmans Publishing Company, all rights reserved; "Opening a Wardrobe: Clyde Kilby (1902–1986)" by Mark Noll, *Reformed Journal*, December 1986, reprinted by permission of the William B. Eerdmans Publishing Company, all rights reserved; "David Wells: The Stability of Grace" by Mark Noll, reprinted with permission in a modified version from the February 7–14, 1990, issue of the *Christian Century*. Copyright © 1990 by the *Christian Century*.

Some material in chapter 5 is taken from "Deep and Wide: How My Mind Has Changed" by Mark Noll, reprinted with permission in a modified version from the June 1, 2010, issue of the *Christian Century*. Copyright © 2010 by the *Christian Century*.

Material in chapter 10 is adapted from Mark Noll, "The Potential of Missiology for the Crises of History," in *History and the Christian Historian*, ed. Ronald Wells. Reprinted by permission of the William B. Eerdmans Publishing Company. All rights reserved.

14   15   16   17   18   19   20   7   6   5   4   3   2   1

In Memoriam
Francis and Evelyn Noll
Donald L. Andersen

Contents

Introduction

To ask a historian for an autobiographical memoir risks replicating the absurdity of a famous Monty Python sketch entitled "Novel Writing: Thomas Hardy." It features three minutes of breathless blather from a play-by-play announcer who, assisted by a ponderously earnest color commentator, describes Thomas Hardy penning the first sentence of *The Return of the Native*: "The crowd grows quiet now as Hardy settles himself down at the desk, body straight, shoulders relaxed, pen held lightly but firmly in the right hand, he dips the pen in the ink, and he's off . . ."[1]

For the most part, historians sit, read books, prepare lectures, grade student papers, occasionally travel to archives, sit some more, organize notes and books, relax by going to museums (and reading everything on all of the placards), attend conferences to hear papers read, write books and articles, retire, read some more, and fade away. The constant effort to figure out why people, institutions, ideas, cultural assumptions, conflicts, social relationships, and day-to-day living developed as they did in the past leaves little time or psychic energy for close attention to ourselves. While some of the books that historians write might be lively, humane, and compelling, our lives rarely are.

1. "Monty Python—Novel Writing," YouTube, http://www.youtube.com/watch?v=ogPZ5CY9KoM, accessed July 2, 2013.

There are a few exceptions. Samuel Eliot Morison not only wrote the official history of the US Navy during World War II but was himself a fine amateur sailor and a naval officer on active duty during that conflict. Paul Fussell was just getting started on a career as a literary historian that would lead to very impressive books on the experience of participants in both world wars when he was drafted for battle in the Pacific. M. A. Polievktov, a distinguished historian working in St. Petersburg, witnessed firsthand crucial events of the Russian Revolution in early 1917 and then organized a series of revealing interviews with key participants right on the spot.[2] And sometimes academic historians have been called from the library and the classroom to become college provosts or presidents, where they are forced to act instead of just observing others in action. But these are exceptions that prove the rule.

Yet what are friends for if not to push you to do things you would otherwise not even consider? In this case, Joel Carpenter of Calvin College's Nagel Institute for the Study of World Christianity and Robert Hosack of Baker Academic were working on a scheme with a worthy purpose. Because they are deeply impressed with how dramatically the shape of world Christianity has changed over the last century, they are trying to find innovative ways to communicate the significance of those changes. They have concluded that minds click off and eyes glaze over when audiences are simply assaulted with the numbers measuring those changes. However impressive, such numbers can come off like recitations of the national debt or the trade imbalance with China. Yet they also feel that if more believers worship Sunday by Sunday in the Congo than in Canada, if churches in China are fuller than churches in Europe, if missionaries from Brazil, Korea, and Nigeria are becoming more numerous than missionaries from the "Christian West," then it is important to understand how, where, and why Christianity has become the first truly global religion.

2. Samuel Eliot Morison, *History of the United States Naval Operations in World War II*, 15 vols. (Boston: Little, Brown, 1947–62); Paul Fussell, *Wartime: Understanding and Behavior in the Second World War* (New York: Oxford University Press, 1989); Semion Lyandres, *The Fall of Tsarism: Untold Stories of the February 1917 Revolution* (New York: Oxford University Press, 2013).

Joel and Bob also concluded that only fragments of the literate public could be enticed to read books about individuals, organizations, and developments in the Majority Christian World (Africa, Latin America, and Asia)—if the names, places, and events are unfamiliar—regardless of how objectively important these people and events might be. Thankfully, solidly researched books are now proliferating about such important people, significant events, and places where Christian faith now thrives.[3] Much of what these books reveal is almost certainly more important for the future of Christianity than most of the people and events that we in the West recognize from our own recent history. Yet because these people and events remain outside the orbit of familiarity, it is hard for publishers to attract readers for books about them.

But maybe, Joel and Bob reasoned, a few more readers might pay attention to personal accounts of how some of us who are securely nestled in American settings nonetheless came to share their conviction about the tremendous significance of the new worlds of Christianity. As a result of such thinking, they conceived the series of which this book is a part.

To me, they posed this challenge: would I write a personal narrative to describe the process by which I came to share their belief that full attention to the non-Western world had become essential for any responsible grasp of the history of Christianity. They knew that I was trained as a conventional student of Western church history, which has traditionally concentrated on European and American developments or, when taking notice of the Majority World, has done so in terms of missionary efforts from the West. They also knew that for the last several decades my day job has been to teach, research, and write books on topics in American history. How, they wondered, did you become interested in reading about non-Western developments? Why did you plan and then begin to teach courses on world Christian history? What led you to write books aimed at general audiences about some aspects of that history?

---

3. Reviews of many of them, along with much other useful material, appear regularly in the *International Bulletin of Missionary Research* (*IBMR*).

Despite my grave suspicion about personal memoir as a genre and real reluctance to become introspective, I agreed. Why? Because for a person with historical instincts, the effort to grasp how Christianity came to exist as it does in the world today just seems very important as a puzzle begging to be explained. But that is not all. In the course of reading, teaching, and trying to write about the recent world history of Christianity, it also became obvious that this new knowledge spoke directly to the experiential and theological realities of Christian faith itself. When those realities are the most important things in your own life, it is natural to want to learn how others have experienced the presence of Christ and understood truths of the faith—even if those others have lived in situations very different from my own. And still more. As someone called to function as a scholar, it has long seemed to me imperative that at least some Christian believers should be thinking hard about why and how Christian believers should be thinking hard. As it turned out, trying to understand the new dimensions of world Christianity has proven to be a natural extension of efforts to encourage myself and others to pursue intellectual life as a calling from God.[4]

For these reasons and more, Joel and Bob won me over. If I could communicate something about the sheer pleasure of expanded historical understanding, the encouragement for deepened Christian life and thought from learning about Majority World Christianity, and the spur to thinking like a Christian that these new ventures opened up, it might be worth the effort.

❖

My title for this book comes not only from Scripture but also from recent world history. Several times in the book of Revelation the same words appear to describe both the entire human race and the redeemed children of God. In various combinations—sometimes in plural form, sometimes singular—the words are "nation," "tribe," "language," and "people." Biblical scholars can parse the exact meaning of these

4. Explored in *The Scandal of the Evangelical Mind* (Grand Rapids: Eerdmans, 1994) and *Jesus Christ and the Life of the Mind* (Grand Rapids: Eerdmans, 2011).

four terms, but it seems obvious that they are meant to describe the widest possible linguistic, ethnic, political, familial, racial, historical, and social diversity.

The most dramatic of these passages appears in chapter 5 where the key actor is called "the Lion of the Tribe of Judah," "the Root of David," and "the Lamb" who was slain. When this One opens a scroll that no one else can approach, "four living creatures" and "twenty-four elders" sing a new song:

> You are worthy to take the scroll
>> and to open its seals,
> for you were slaughtered and by your blood you ransomed for
>> God
>> saints from every tribe and language and people and
>>> nation;
> you have made them to be a kingdom and priests serving our
>> God,
>> and they will reign on earth. (Rev. 5:9–10)

From this passage we learn that when the finished work of Christ is, in the other sense of the term, finished, his kingdom will be made up of people from everywhere, speaking all imaginable languages, shaped by greatly different historical experiences, representing every conceivable social location, and appearing as a rainbow of "red and yellow, black and white."

The lesson for a historian from this passage would seem to be obvious. If the people of God come from every tribe and nation, so then should a history of the people of God try to take in every tribe and nation. Of course, since historians are far from divine, they can never describe the church from God's universal perspective. Yet to realize that the Christian story, properly considered, must always be moving farther out to take in more of the "kingdom and priests serving our God" is now essential, even when historians work on only one aspect of one strand of the tribes, languages, peoples, or nations.

Alongside the mandate for history in this biblical passage, the recent past contains many events that anticipate the Revelator's view of the

End. One of the most telling of these events took place on Whitsunday
in 1862, when five thousand South Sea Islanders from Tonga, Fiji, and
Samoa gathered to inaugurate a new specifically Christian government with a professedly Christian king. They marked this auspicious
occasion by singing a hymn that had become the missionary beacon
of the evangelical movement.[5] Developments in the Pacific that led to
that day had included some of the evil effects of Western imperialism—families disrupted, resources stolen, women ravished, fire arms
introduced. Yet despite the Islanders' experience with those evils,
they were able to sift through what they had learned from European
contact and chose—for themselves—the hymn for the day.

That hymn was Isaac Watts's Christianized version of the Seventy-
Second Psalm. To quote it here, with all of the verses that Watts wrote,
might offend modern sensibilities (especially because of its reference
to "barbarous nations").[6] But a full quotation also conveys Watts's
grasp of how wide the kingdom of God really is. It also suggests how
poignant it must have been for these islanders "with their kings" to
know that they too belonged among the "people and realms of every
tongue."

> Jesus shall reign where'er the sun
> Doth his successive journeys run;
> His Kingdom stretch from shore to shore,
> Till moons shall wax and wane no more.
>
> Behold the islands with their kings,
> And Europe her best tribute brings;
> From North to South the princes meet
> To pay their homage at his feet.
>
> There Persia glorious to behold,
> There India shines in eastern gold;
> And barbarous nations at his word
> Submit and bow and own their Lord.

5. Christopher Idle, *Stories of Our Favorite Hymns* (Grand Rapids: Eerdmans,
1980), 24.

6. Isaac Watts, *The Psalms of David Imitated in the Language of the New Testament, and Apply'd to the Christian State and Worship* (London, 1719), 186–87.

For him shall endless prayer be made,
And princes throng to crown his head,
His name like sweet perfume shall rise
With every morning sacrifice.

People and realms of every tongue
Dwell on his love with sweetest song;
And infant voices shall proclaim
Their early blessings on his name.

Blessings abound where'er He reigns,
The prisoner leaps to lose his chains,
The weary find eternal rest,
And all the sons of want are blest.

Where He displays His healing power
Death and the curse are known no more;
In Him the tribes of Adam boast
More blessings than their father lost.

Let every creature rise and bring
Peculiar honors to our King;
Angels descend with songs again,
And earth repeat the loud Amen.

To quote this great hymn here does one thing more. It anticipates a theme that will appear later in the book when we consider the unusual importance that singing the praises of God has enjoyed in almost all Christian communities. Significantly, however, if singing has been universal among believers, the varieties of music sung have been highly particular, culturally specific, and often unintelligible to outsiders.

❖

My bosses, Carpenter and Hosack, have insisted that this book be personal and anecdotal, and that it not be festooned with too many footnotes that are otherwise second nature for a self-respecting historian. They suggested that short, impressionistic chapters would be better than the ponderous, complex sort. They also indicated that it would be fine to excerpt or repeat fragments of material I had originally written for other purposes. To assuage my scholarly conscience, I do note when I am revising here what has been published elsewhere. Otherwise, I have tried to obey orders.

Left to myself, I would probably have begun this account in the late 1960s when I was coming to learn about a form of Christianity quite different from the one in which I had been raised and which played an important part in fixing my course as an adult believer. Or perhaps in the late 1980s when in fairly rapid succession I first heard Andrew Walls lecture and then was induced by good friends at Wheaton College to take part in a summer teaching expedition to Oradea, Romania. But my wife, Maggie, thinks the story has to begin much earlier. For reasons that should become apparent, I'm sure she is right.

❖ 1 ❖

Cedar Rapids

At Calvary Baptist Church in Cedar Rapids, Iowa, where I grew up, missionaries were conspicuous—both in the flesh and as idealized exemplars of what the Christian life should be. Not only did we stage an annual weeklong missionary conference, with nightly meetings addressed by Christian workers from around the globe who spoke about and illustrated (with slide projectors and curios) their tasks in the Philippines, Brazil, Argentina, India, Pakistan, the Ivory Coast, what was then called the Belgian Congo, Alaska, and more. But other missionaries also regularly passed through, to be introduced on Sunday morning, or more commonly to address the congregation on Sunday evening or at the church's midweek prayer meeting. My parents, Francis and Evelyn Noll, were active in all phases of life at Calvary Baptist and so did their full share of hosting, entertaining, and squiring the visiting missionaries. In later life, long after I had left the family nest, my parents took several tours to missionary sites where on the ground in Africa, Pakistan, the Philippines, and perhaps elsewhere, they reconnected with missionaries who had come through Cedar Rapids.

During the 1950s and early 1960s I was not in a great position to appreciate the mission-mindedness of our local church. But much later, a little bit of family history played its part in clearing up my vision. My father, a navy pilot in the Second World War, had flown eighty-nine missions off his carrier to support the movement of US troops westward across the Pacific. More than three decades after that service—and because contact with missionaries had helped redirect his life—one of these tours took my father to sites in the Philippines that he had once flown over in his Grumman TBF Avenger. I was greatly struck with what the passage of time had brought about and keen to learn more about his wartime experiences, but he seemed more impressed by the chance to meet Filipino believers and view missionary life up close.

In the late 1980s, when I began to realize how important the world as a whole actually was for the history of Christianity, I felt that these new insights had to overcome what I had experienced of missionaries when growing up. At that later time I was, for example, much impressed with books that explained the irreversibility of translation— once missionaries and their native coworkers had translated the Bible, Scripture no longer belonged to the missionaries but was put to use for purposes determined by those who spoke the target language. Thus, the missionary translators might want new converts to concentrate on the apostle Paul's account of the substitutionary atonement, but the converts themselves might view the struggle between Elijah and the prophets of Baal, or the genealogy of Matthew 1, as the key to the whole biblical story. The process of translation, my new reading revealed, was far from the uncomplicated task of "bringing the good news" that I remembered the missionaries describe.

What I was learning in the late 1980s also showed clearly that the great surge in world Christian adherence was taking place primarily through the efforts of native teachers, local "Bible women," colporteurs, and newly converted catechists and evangelists. Missionaries often provided a spark for this process of indigenization, but it was almost always local believers who fanned the spark into flame. In addition, I was learning more about the costs of conversion: stories of missionary deprivation, even martyrdom, stuck in my memory from what I had heard as a youth; but broader reading revealed that what local believers sacrificed for their faith in many new Christian regions—property, health, family relationships, even life itself—was almost always much more extensive than what missionaries had been asked to endure.

The young people of our church, along with adults and youth everywhere in evangelical America, were deeply moved in January 1956 as news spread about the five young missionaries killed by the native Waorani in an Ecuadorian jungle. When a memorable book written by one of the widows appeared shortly thereafter, their sacrifice made an even deeper impression. That book, Elisabeth Elliot's *Shadow of the Almighty: The Life and Testimony of Jim Elliot* (Harper, 1958), deserves its status as a classic of evangelical spiritual biography. Yet I do not remember any comparable books, or serious attention of any sort, paid to the thousands of Majority World Christians who in those very years were experiencing hardship, deprivation, and often death for their Christian adherence: Kenyan believers targeted by Mau Maus, Mexican Pentecostals attacked for violating village traditions, Chinese Christians of all sorts rounded up in the early years of the Mao regime. On rare occasions, there might be mention of believers suffering for Christ in China or the Soviet Union—but usually to illustrate a larger problem: the threat of godless communism. From time to time there might also be reports of Protestants persecuted in Colombia—but again to underscore a more general danger: the ongoing threat posed to "real Christianity" by the domineering actions of the Catholic Church.

With most of my generation of evangelical young people, I also thrilled to stories about the self-sacrificing martyrdom of John and Betty Stam, even though the only concrete circumstance respecting their lives that I remember is that they were slain by Chinese Reds. In fact, they were killed in 1934 as a by-product of a long and complicated civil war, whose origins could be traced to the failed Chinese republic of Sun Yat-sen, or back further to the Boxer Rebellion of 1900, or perhaps even to the Opium Wars of the 1830s when Britain muscled its way into the China trade by allowing the East India Company to market narcotics to the Chinese people. The Stams' story had the potential for illuminating the history of that part of the world where they met their end, but I recall only an emphasis on the kind of piety we were supposed to emulate.

In other words, a serious disconnect separated what I remembered about missionary service from my youth and what decades later I was learning about the dynamics of world Christianity.

In retrospect, it is clear that the problem was not primarily with the missionaries I met, for most of them were dedicated people, and almost all of them bore lightly the weight of commitment that took them from North America to "the regions beyond." Instead, part of my problem was missionary hagiography. At least as I perceived the matter, our species of hagiography had little room for critical, particular, or concrete thought. In the apparent hierarchy of godliness, missionary service was not like other vocations. The names of missionaries who began service but then moved on to other careers were expunged from the congregation's memory as thoroughly as anti-Stalinists once vanished from Marxist photographs documenting the history of the Soviet Union. The missionary aura seemed to convey a level of sanctity on those who continued in the harness that removed them from the realm of merely terrestrial concern.

Yet precisely in those early years, I was growing increasingly interested in terrestrial concerns. To be sure, I was also reading heaps of stories about Ty Cobb, Babe Ruth, Dizzy Dean, Lou Gehrig, Ted Williams, and other heroes of the baseball diamond who somehow escaped my aversion to hagiography. But there were even more books about the nation's founding, the Civil War, the notable presidents and statesmen, Indians and settlers on the frontier, the Depression, and the world wars. This reading was introducing me to political conflicts, material interests, imperial aspirations, colonial resistance, and this-worldly complexity. And with these dimensions of human experience I was fascinated. Another disconnect followed: between the new worlds opened by such reading and the worlds I remember from early attention to missionaries.

Our missionaries were treated like gods, and gods, it seemed, could not be bothered with merely human questions of politics, culture, economics, literature, foreign policy, or the comparative study of religion. In point of fact, I now know that some of the very missionaries who passed through our church did have definite, and sometimes learned, opinions on these questions. If I had asked them about broader cultural or theological matters, some of them would have provided thoughtfully informative answers. But for whatever reason, their interest in such matters and my eagerness to learn about the shape of the world never quite connected.

The reading urged upon us was another part of the problem. To be sure, juvenile missionary literature had some points in its favor. At about age ten or eleven, I devoured the *Jungle Doctor* books by the Australian Paul White. (When many years later I discovered some of these old books and read one or two to our own children, I found them not quite as good as I thought they were when I was ten but a lot better than I would have considered them if I had rediscovered them at age twenty-five instead of nearly twice twenty-five.)

Graduating to what was heralded as more serious missionary literature created the really serious problems, though I should be charitable in recognizing the purposes for which such books were written. Besides the unbelievable heights of spiritual dedication portrayed in these volumes, what particularly put me off was what I perceived as insensitivity to local contexts, a lack of interest in historical background, the absence of attention to cultural connections, and a distressing absence of maps.

One particular example sticks in my mind, although my memory of this book may be a product of late-adolescent prejudice. Whatever the cause, I can still remember the distaste with which I finished a biography of James Outram Fraser entitled *Behind the Ranges*. At least as I recall it, the book furnished very little on the texture of the South China world in which Fraser worked, almost nothing that would allow a reader to situate the Lisu people in broader ethnic, linguistic, or political contexts, no analysis of family or economic life, little attention to the history of China or Britain, and only sparse details about Chinese culture or the culture from which Fraser had come. Recently I discovered that the original 1944 edition of this work did in fact contain maps, but I am pretty sure that the copy I read was as mapless as it could be. Later I also discovered that Fraser had been a pioneer in recording and analyzing the Lisu language, but these aspects of his work had also escaped my attention.

The sad result of experiences with books like *Behind the Ranges* was that, just as I was beginning to get serious about other kinds of history generally, and soon other kinds of church history specifically, I abandoned mission history as in any way relevant to those developing historical interests. Mea culpa. Mea maxima culpa.

❖

It took quite a while to recognize the mistakes I made—about the importance of missionaries and about my own experiences at Calvary Baptist. The perception of an outsider was crucial to that recognition.

The outsider was my wife—though when she first visited Cedar Rapids, she was still only a girlfriend. Maggie Packer had been raised in a conservative Presbyterian church where missionaries were not unknown but where they occupied a smaller place in the spiritual universe than at Calvary Baptist. Her experience was especially different from mine in one crucial respect. Missionaries in her denomination received their financial backing from the denomination. Missionaries visiting Cedar Rapids were, among other activities, raising their own support. At the time I did not realize that our Baptist pattern was becoming increasingly common throughout the world, while the older Presbyterian model represented a legacy of traditional Christendom that was becoming less and less important as the twentieth-century Christian world emerged.

When Maggie first sat down for a meal in our home, what leapt out at her—literally in front of her face—were pins affixed to a big map on the wall. The map covered one entire side of the family dining area; the pins, obviously, represented the missionaries whom our church supported or who were otherwise known to the family. For several missionary conferences, my father had helped construct even larger maps above the church's baptistery, which at Calvary Baptist occupied the prominent ecclesiastical space where crucifixes hang in more liturgical churches. These maps at church were decorated with tiny light bulbs identifying the location of the church's missionaries. The maps always presented the Mercator Projection, with North America and Europe "up" and Western Europe in the center, although at the time I was completely inert to the way in which maps convey a story about what is central and what is peripheral in world history.

In retrospect, I also am remembering that our missionary conferences functioned as an alternative liturgy. They often took place on the week between Palm Sunday and Easter, which meant that when traditional liturgical churches were observing foundational elements of the Christian past, our missionary-minded congregation was looking forward to the Christian future.

Sometime in the late 1950s, my dad built a slightly smaller map, though without electrification, for home. "And you think your interest in world Christianity," Maggie has said to me, "came from reading books by Lamin Sanneh or hearing Andrew Walls lecture or having to make up a new course? I think it started way, way before then."

❖

Prompted by such biographical assistance, it has become increasingly clear that experiences at Calvary Baptist planted seeds that later sprouted as my interest in world Christianity. At least three matters were important.

First was simple awareness. Cedar Rapids was not, I believe, unusually insular by comparison with other Midwestern communities of the 1950s and early 1960s. We knew that employment at our large Quaker Oats plant depended on exports, as well as local climate and national farm policy, and that business at Collins Radio picked up considerably when technological competition with the Soviets heated up after the launch of Sputnik in 1957. Excellent teachers in the Cedar Rapids public school system taught us well in the classics of American and English literature, and also provided a solid basis in world and American history. Yet few in that setting were being exposed to as much of the world at large as those of us who, without realizing what was happening, attended even casually to the parade of missionaries passing through.

Even if missionary presentations were overwhelmingly pious in tone and almost entirely apolitical, still, who in Cedar Rapids knew anything about conditions in the Argentine pampas, or could locate the Ivory Coast on an African map, or heard firsthand about the paralyzing heat of summer in the plains of India, or learned what it was like to experience the sudden end of colonial rule in the Congo—unless they were exposed to visiting missionaries. Progressive academics for several decades have been attacking with great intensity the role of missionaries in promoting the evils of Western imperialism; recently a range of observers, including anthropologists and historians with no personal stake in Christian faith, have countered with what should have been obvious all along. However missionaries measured up against what has now become the accepted moral norm for respect of non-Western cultures, in the context of former times—and compared to all other agents out of the West—missionaries were always among the most humane, most altruistic, and most self-critical representatives of Western nations in non-Western regions. Similarly, viewed in strictly comparative terms, very few middle-class young people from small-city Iowa of my generation were introduced to as many places far, far away from the United States as were the youth of churches like Calvary Baptist that were committed to the missionary proclamation of the gospel.

This exposure to missionaries also worked at some level to influence the course that family members took. Why was my brother Craig so fascinated by foreign languages, and myself only slightly less so? Why did it seem so natural for him to spend a summer with missionaries in Alaska or later to enlist for service in Turkey with the Peace Corps? My sister, Ann, would probably be the best person to answer such questions, if they can be answered. I'm pretty sure she would say that somewhere in our family's history there has to be a large place for early experience with missionaries.

The second thing that prompted my interest in world Christianity was an introduction to the dynamics of cross-cultural communication. Visiting missionaries, so far as I can recall, never uttered the words "indigenization" or "enculturation"; they did not dwell on foreign political systems, except to point out how strange some of them were by American standards; they rarely spoke, in our Baptist setting, about the difficulty of planting denominational churches where Western denominations were unknown. But they did let on how difficult it could be to learn Asian or African languages far removed from English; they did relate struggles and breakthroughs in communicating with native helpers; they did show slides that depicted, sometimes dramatically, how far from home their labors took them; they occasionally presented samples of native music that did not sound anything like the gospel tunes or traditional Protestant hymnody we sang; and they certainly communicated something about their "cultural distance" from a small city in the Midwest, though not by using that phrase.

Once again, seeds were going into the ground. It would take much nurture for a harvest to appear, but a hint had been provided, awaiting later development, that the Christian faith itself began, and has constantly existed, as a cross-cultural faith.

The third vital contribution from those early years was the Christianity that spurred missionary motivation—for the missionaries themselves, but much more for the Calvary faithful who placed such a high value on the missionary enterprise. I suppose outside observers would have been correct to view our church as "fundamentalist." We had the long sermon series on the prophetic future detailed in the book of Revelation; we either sponsored or took part in well-organized revival campaigns; at the end of almost every service, we imitated Billy Graham by featuring altar calls to the accompaniment of "Just as I am, without one plea"; we disapproved of smoking, drinking, movies, and other signs of worldliness; and, although many of us had close Catholic friends, we knew there was something very wrong with Catholicism itself.

Yet if "fundamentalism" means angry zealots on the warpath, there was virtually none of that. Instead, we had a patient, loving pastor, Don Andersen, who went out of his way to stand with the needy, the grieving, the injured, and the weak. We enjoyed youth pastors who, despite occasional flashes of immaturity, really liked kids. And most important, the church was full of laymen and laywomen who exemplified mature, balanced Christian faith. There were the dedicated teachers who made Sunday school a time of friendship as well as (occasional) learning. There were the stalwarts on the church softball team who taught hot-headed youth that losing was not the worst thing in the world. There was the young church secretary with whom all the teenaged boys were at least half in love and who tolerated the most boorish behavior from her admirers with infectious good humor. There were those who went "calling" on Thursday nights to ask visitors where they would spend eternity if they died that night and sometimes also provided a little material help for folks in need. There were the elderly who bore infirmities, poverty, loneliness, and sometimes alienation from children with remarkably few complaints.

Calvary Baptist was by no means heaven on earth. Yet even if—as I might now conclude—the Christianity on offer was too little interested in culture, too unconcerned about history, too much guided by formulaic piety, and too thin in its theology, it was genuine all the way down. Depth of conviction fueled the fixation on missionary service. Of course, we heard regularly that every Christian should be "one sent," but we knew who really took that admonition to heart. Missionaries were the exemplars, and for me they helped crack open the world.

❖ 2 ❖

Rescued by the Reformation

I f it were necessary to review comprehensively the years between going off to college and early adulthood, I would have to write about many things. For awareness of Christian faith as a genuinely world religion, however, the key development was certainly the process that moved me from interested Christian spectator to committed Christian participant. The other things, in order of importance, were finding a spouse with whom it has been a singular privilege to share the comforts and vicissitudes of life; sensing that an ideal vocation would involve reading, writing, and teaching about the past; coming to realize that I resonated with plot, narrative, and change over time much more than with static relationships or questions of truth shorn of context; and giving up the adolescent conviction that burying jump shots, scooping up grounders, and sinking long putts were of nearly ultimate significance.

The movement from spectator to participant occurred as my disquiet about the religion with which I had grown up gave way to a captivating new experience of Christian faith. Yet important qualifications must be stated before trying to describe that change. Now fifty years removed from late adolescence, I am aware of much distortion. I know that my perception of the teaching and attitudes I experienced cannot possibly do justice to what an objective, disinterested account would record. If there were faults in that upbringing, the responsibility doubtless belonged much more to myself than to anyone else. In addition, what I describe in the following paragraphs surely falsifies what actually happened by compressing into a short span of years insights that developed much more gradually—that, in fact, are developing still.

Yet with bias fully in view, a crude statement of how I would read my own life goes as follows. From internalizing much preaching about what I needed to do in order to be saved, I experienced existentially Martin Luther's message about what God had endured in order to save me. From a view of the Bible preoccupied by its meaning for the future, I learned from John Calvin a way of reading Scripture that revealed its pervasive relevance for the present. From singing true, but thin, words about the wonderful grace of Jesus, I was transformed by singing Charles Wesley's account of a long-imprisoned spirit unchained by the bright light of divine mercy. From being taught that I should be intensely concerned about how many authors contributed to the book of Isaiah, I followed Jonathan Edwards in seeing that the only really important question was the purpose for which God created the world (it was for his own glory). Just a little bit later, from seeking first one and then another foundation, it was reassuring beyond comprehension to hear in the Heidelberg Catechism that "my only comfort in life and in death is my faithful Savior Jesus Christ who has fully paid for all my sins with his precious blood."

In other words, the riches of classical Protestantism opened a new and exceedingly compelling vision of existence. Intellectually, theologically, existentially, I was rescued by the Reformation.

The contrast between what I had experienced in my home church as well as at evangelical Wheaton College, where I was an undergraduate from 1964 to 1968, and what I was learning from classical Protestant sources was almost certainly not as stark as I perceived at the time. There was certainly more grace in my mid-twentieth-century neo-evangelical world and certainly more unresolved tension in the religion of Luther, Calvin, Wesley, and Edwards than I thought. Yet at the time the contrast seemed dramatic.

Intellectually considered, American evangelicalism of the 1960s offered a halfway house still painfully situated between the burdens of fundamentalism and the confident world-and-life affirmations of traditional trinitarian Christianity. I am now convinced that many of my evangelical pastors and teachers really did know that questions of biblical inerrancy were only important because of the Scriptures' message of divine grace, or more generally that an all-or-nothing concentration on epistemological questions, argued with fierce reliance on ostensibly scientific factuality, had the effect of obscuring the very gospel such efforts were supposed to protect. It was probably also true that the theological preoccupations of many evangelicals were not as far removed as they seemed from truly basic Christian essentials.

As I would put it now, those essential tasks included probing the meaning of the Trinity in order to discern the basic meaning of human existence, pondering the paradoxical beauties of Christ's substitutionary death for sinners, asking how the life of Christ might shape the daily life of believers, and exploring what the divine creation of nature and the providential direction of human cultures entailed for faithful Christian living. Instead, I remember an awful lot of attention to less consequential matters: salvation presented as a one-time transaction initiated by my own efforts, concern for history reduced to predicting the end of time, an interest in nature limited to assertions about when God created the world, and endless and often fanciful arguments wielding Bible verses ripped out of the larger contexts of Scripture. These latter preoccupations might have arisen from efforts to major on the majors, but I experienced them as a lot of sweating about the small stuff.

Spiritually considered, the situation was even more dire. Like everyone else in young adulthood—indeed, like everyone else period—I needed to be liberated from chains forged by the lust of the eyes, the lust of the flesh, and the pride of life. To expand on the wording from 1 John 2:16, I was desperate to be freed from defining myself in relation to how I stood with others, from allowing natural appetites to become self-destructive "pleasures," and from thinking that I really was the center of the universe. The evangelical Christianity I experienced was certainly alert to these great challenges. But for reasons that memoirs by former evangelicals and chastened evangelicals have fully explored, a religion ostensibly defined by grace could be experienced as being tightly bound by law.

At least from my angle, the remedies offered from within the evangelical world to humankind's moral diseases—diseases portrayed so forcefully in the Scriptures that evangelicals exalted so highly—fell short. Part of the problem was what seemed to be taught as ideals for holy living. These ideals were tightly limited. I was not alone as a young person in hearing that godliness meant not smoking, drinking, or going to movies, and waiting for sex until marriage—a particularly nasty bit of confusion that, in later years, meant that as evangelicals lightened up on drink and film we have also lightened up on marital fidelity. The weightier matters of the law—doing justice, loving mercy, walking humbly with God—were not entirely disregarded, but were all too easily obscured by the behavioral shibboleths of fundamentalism. As for the notion that political life, artistic endeavor, academic work, or business activity might actually be carried out as a believer's sacrifice of praise—these were largely unexplored possibilities.

The most important spiritual problem was that, despite endless repetition about the fullness of God's grace, it was all too easy to absorb an image of Christianity defined almost entirely by what you did or did not do, entirely equated with a short list of propositions that had to be believed, or practically reduced to my conversion experience and the need to convert others.

It was certainly not mistaken to learn that divine grace and the good deeds of a moral life were intimately connected. Neither was it wrong to believe that dogmatic assertions played an important role in properly functioning Christianity. Nor was it improper to contend for the reality of conversion. To quote the Canadian historian George Rawlyk, about whom more will be written below, "Religious conversions have actually occurred; peoples' lives have apparently been profoundly and permanently changed. . . . Conversions still take place and so do religious revivals."[1]

It was, instead, a mistake to leave the impression that moral behavior constituted Christian faith. It was also a mistake to think that my checklist of proper beliefs amounted to Christianity as such. And it was a mistake to let the reality of conversion crowd out other Christian realities.

The result of such misplaced emphasis was a practical approach to life filled with certainties that were never ridiculous, and never unconnected to living faith, but that were also dangerously partial. There were quite a few of them.

- In the roster of sins, the most grievous were unwed pregnancy, divorce, alcoholism, and homosexual acts (about which we knew very little in that more sheltered time); next came open dishonesty, cursing, racism, and indictable legal offences; priggishness, gluttony, gossip, and pharisaism brought up the distant rear.
- Conversion meant a dramatic turn from sin and self—mobsters, athletes, and pagans on the mission field were the ideal types—and only rarely meant slowly nurtured growth in grace.
- The way of salvation meant coming forward to the front after a church service or revival meeting to receive Christ as personal Savior.
- Catholics were doomed because they followed not Christ, but the pope.
- Churches that baptized babies did not understand the biblical command for baptism to follow a profession of faith.
- And so forth.

I have overstated matters here. Whatever flaws I now perceive, there can be no question that the evangelical world of my youth was full of selfless, faithful people leading exemplary lives. As a historian, my conclusion is that the shocks of contemporary life (which for my parents' generation included the economic uncertainties of the Depression; the

---

1. George A. Rawlyk, *Wrapped Up in God: A Study of Several Canadian Revivals and Revivalists* (Burlington, ON: Welch, 1988), ix.

dislocations, deaths, and injuries of world war; and the unprecedented postwar surges in education and wealth) combined in a particularly disruptive way with the traumas of fundamentalist-modernist strife and the culture's steady abandonment of once commonly accepted Christian conventions. That combination led to distortions of the faith as communicated by American evangelicals, yet never so severe as to rule out the possibility of deeply authentic Christian life.

Nonetheless, for whatever historical reasons, the Christian message I received from this context seemed very strong on law and disconcertingly ambiguous about grace. At least some of our pastors and revivalists were immensely entertaining, especially as they drew on rich reserves of stories, illustrations, anecdotes, quotations, sayings, and alliterated points to prayerfully ponder. Yet no one in my hearing ever quoted anything like the letter that Martin Luther wrote to his young colleague, Philip Melanchthon, in August 1521:

> Be a sinner and sin boldly, but believe in Christ even more boldly, for he is victorious over sin, death, and the world. As long as we are here . . . we have to sin. . . . It is enough that by the riches of God's glory we have come to know the Lamb that takes away the sin of the world. No sin will separate us from the Lamb, even though we commit fornication and murder a thousand times a day. So you think that the purchase price that was paid for the redemption of our sins by so great a Lamb is too small? Pray boldly—you too are a mighty sinner.[2]

When I was in my early twenties, I was being rescued by such a message.

At this late date, I see more clearly the limits to what at the time appeared simply liberating. Luther's hyperbole could easily lead astray. Theologians quite properly label his wild statement about "a thousand times a day" as "antinomianism," or criticize his apparent disregard for the proper connection between faith and a moral life. In addition,

2. *Letters I*, vol. 48 of Luther's *Works*, ed. Gottfried G. Krodel (Philadelphia: Fortress, 1963), 282.

Luther's enthusiasm for the work of God in the cross could leave little energy for pondering the work of God in the world at large (a standard complaint that we Calvinists make about Lutherans). His outsized personality caused him to run off at the mouth. And the certainty with which Luther stated his positions led some of his spiritual descendants to confuse his dicta with Scripture itself. Yet about the gospel as opened by Martin Luther, if not for every detail of his life and influence, I continue to have no doubts.

He was not interested in abstract pictures of God.[3] Even conceptions of God that had inspired other great teachers in the Christian church were not Luther's primary concern. He appreciated the God of love who had meant so much to German mystics. He did use some of the things that Thomas Aquinas had said about God's rule over the physical and rational worlds (though he could never bring himself to say anything good about Aquinas, whom he considered, without troubling to read him, a promoter of salvation by mental good works). And he certainly learned much from Augustine, for example, about God as pure moral light and Augustine's depiction of the Trinity as constant divine interaction. But these and other reputable Christian images of God were secondary.

Primary, instead, were the concerns with which Luther ended his famous Ninety-Five Theses from October 1517.

> (94) Christians should be exhorted to be diligent in following Christ, their head, through penalties, death, and hell;
> (95) And thus be confident of entering into heaven through many tribulations rather than through the false security of peace.

Shortly thereafter, Luther's intense engagement with the Epistle of Paul to the Romans, which lay behind the Ninety-Five Theses, inspired a further outburst, this one at an academic convocation: "The person who believes that he can obtain grace by doing what is in him adds sin

---

3. I have abridged and personalized the following paragraphs from *Turning Points: Decisive Moments in the History of Christianity*, 3rd ed. (Grand Rapids: Baker Academic, 2012), 154–62; these pages include full documentation for Luther's words quoted here.

to sin so that he becomes doubly guilty. . . . He deserves to be called a theologian . . . who comprehends the visible and manifest things of God seen through suffering and the cross. . . . A theologian of glory calls evil good and good evil. A theologian of the cross calls the thing what it actually is."

The crucial element in Luther's idea of God was a paradox: to understand the power that made heaven and earth, it was necessary to know the powerlessness that hung on a Roman gibbet. To conceive the moral perfection of deity it was necessary to understand the scandal of a criminal's execution. In Luther's view, Christianity begins with Christ dying for sinners; Christianity becomes a reality in human lives when women and men enter into Christ's death by suffering the destruction of their own pretensions as they stand *coram Deo* (in the very presence of God).

As an instinctive polemicist, Luther also spoke against the mind-set opposed to a theology of the cross, what he called a "theology of glory." This aspect of his teaching spoke to me personally with as much negative force as his exposition of the cross spoke positively. A theology of glory asks people to do what lies within their own power, to be up and doing, in order to gain acceptance from themselves, from fellow humans, and, most importantly, from God. A theology of glory guides humans to think that if we could only discipline ourselves properly, we would finally and ultimately please God. With insidious effect, a theology of glory urges humans to think that what *we* do for God matters most in creating a spiritual life, rather than what God has done for us. It was a message that seemed tailored for me personally.

The cross, for Luther, revealed God's verdict: that no amount of human work could make humanity successful; no amount of diligent study could make humanity truly wise; no amount of human exertion could provide enduring joy. The cross, in sum, was God's everlasting "no" to the most fundamental human idolatry of regarding the self as a god. It was God's final word of condemnation for all efforts to enshrine humanity at the center of existence.

Because these denunciations of a theology of glory seemed so fanatical, so excessive, or what we might today call so counterintuitive,

Luther's "evangelical breakthrough" took him an excruciatingly long time to experience. That painful process, however, helps explain its remarkable effect once announced. For those—like myself—who recognized the pilgrimage of their own hearts in what he wrote, there was great reward. A theology of the cross did not only destroy, it also opened up. Here is how Luther put it:

> For where man's strength ends, God's strength begins, provided faith is present and waits on him. And when the oppression comes to an end, it becomes manifest what great strength was hidden under the weakness. Even so, Christ was powerless on the cross; and yet there he performed his mightiest work and conquered sin, death, world, hell, devil, and all evil. Thus all the martyrs were strong and overcame. Thus, too, all who suffer and are oppressed overcome.

I took Luther to mean that because we humans were not responsible for justifying ourselves before God, we could experience the most complete freedom imaginable. If God, as demonstrated on the cross, was for us, who could be against us? As sinners whom God justified freely by his grace, we were now free to work, play, live, nurture, witness, relax, worship, create, and enjoy—not because we deserved such freedom, but because in Christ we enjoyed all that the Father through the Spirit had bestowed upon the Son.

Such instruction was for me a streak of lightning that illuminated the pathway to life. When I read Luther's very last words, I thought they summarized almost everything: "Wir sind Bettler. Das ist wahr" (We are beggars. That's the truth). This acknowledgment was not a cry of despair, for I knew that because of the cross, God now heard the beggar's cry.

Some years later, after being deeply affected by J. S. Bach's church cantatas, Passions, and Mass in B Minor, it was evident to me why insightful historians like Jaroslav Pelikan claimed that Bach had internalized more of Luther's theology than almost anyone else in history. Bach's masterful counterpoint reflected a musical harmonization of apparently conflicting realities that mirrored the conflicting realities of the cross. Likewise, his exquisite matching of text and music—certainly as artful as any such match in Western musical history—communicated as effectively as humanly possible the great pathos of a suffering God and the all-but-unspeakable joy of liberation in Christ.

Of course it was not "Luther's theology" that inspired Bach or that has been so helpful to so many. Luther would have been the first to say that whatever he saw clearly about the relationship of God to humanity was every bit as much a divine gift as any other true insight we might receive about the life of Christ or the message of Scripture.

In my evangelical tradition, this understanding of the gospel was not entirely foreign. In fact, many of the hymns we sang in Cedar Rapids or at Wheaton College spelled it out with a powerful blend of emotional and cognitive force: "O Sacred Head, Now Wounded" (from the Middle Ages as translated into German by the seventeenth-century Lutheran Paul Gerhardt and then into English by the nineteenth-century Presbyterian James Waddel Alexander); "When I Survey the Wondrous Cross" and "Am I a Soldier of the Cross?" (Isaac Watts); "O For a Thousand Tongues to Sing" (especially the phrase "he breaks the power of canceled sin, he sets the prisoner free"; Charles Wesley); or "Come, Ye Sinners, Poor and Needy" ("Let not conscience make you linger, nor of fitness fondly dream; all the fitness he requireth is to feel your need of him"; Joseph Hart); "Beneath the Cross of Jesus" (Elizabeth Clephane); and even at least partially in "The Old Rugged Cross," despite the singer-centered focus of that gospel song.

Yet in looking back, it seemed as if we sang such hymns and then hurried on—to further behavioral injunctions, deeper suspicion of "the world," increased attention to eccentric biblical interpretations, and ever more restricted focus on the conversion experience. The theology of the great hymns remained potent but too often obscured by what else was going on.

I have recently read what Douglas Sweeney wrote about his awakening due to Luther's influence. This also is my story: "Luther helped me understand the gospel message in its purity. He showed me that God granted saving faith because of Christ, not for (sinful) earnestness. I only had to receive this precious gift and thank the Lord. I gained assurance of my faith, stopped my spiritual navel gazing, and began to get over myself."[4]

❖

Rambling on at such length about a spiritual journey undertaken entirely within Western contexts—in a memoir focused on world Christianity—requires a word of explanation. During the years of early adulthood I found a resolution to dilemmas manufactured within contemporary American evangelicalism by absorbing insights from early-modern European Protestantism. This transition does not seem to have much to do with the world at large. Indeed, at the time I was entirely oblivious to how any of this experience might bear on the broader history of Christianity. I knew, and probably cared, almost nothing about the truly important developments that were taking place in that wider sphere while I was heeding Martin Luther: Chinese churches outlawed during Mao Zedong's Great Proletarian Cultural Revolution of 1966–76, and not only surviving but actually in some instances flourishing; valiant bishops standing up to the murderous Idi Amin in Uganda; black, mixed-race, and a few white believers putting theology to work as they opposed the apartheid regime in South Africa; Pentecostalism and other forms of charismatic Christianity beginning to take off in Brazil, Nicaragua, and other regions of Latin America; and the effects of the Second Vatican Council beginning to embroil and transform Catholics worldwide. By 1974 and the publicity that appeared in *Christianity Today* and other evangelical publications about the Lausanne Congress on World Evangelization, I was beginning to pay attention, but just barely.

The connection to world Christianity lay in the shape of my experience. It was a discovery resulting from cross-cultural contact. Viewing the gospel from another's perspective allowed me, for the first time, really to see the gospel. If that other perspective came from across time instead of across space, it still meant that I was

4. Douglas A. Sweeney, "Why I Am an Evangelical and a Lutheran," in *Why We Belong: Evangelical Unity and Denominational Diversity*, ed. A. L. Chute, C. W. Morgan, and R. A. Peterson (Wheaton: Crossway, 2013), 118.

learning about myself and my environment by attending to others who lived in considerably different times and places. To my eternal benefit, I had discovered how much could be gained from subjecting taken-for-granted spiritual convictions to criticism far from home. In other words, I had discovered the truth of the saying that Wikipedia informs me was first uttered in a novel by L. P. Hartley: "The past is a foreign country: they do things differently there."

It was a first step toward realizing that "they" might also do things differently elsewhere in the here and now.

❖ 3 ❖

First Teachers

Friends and family showed great forbearance in not asking too frequently, "Still in school yet?" as my career as a student continued through the 1960s and early 1970s. After graduating with a major in English from Wheaton in 1968, I studied comparative literature for two years at the University of Iowa, church history for two years at Trinity Evangelical Divinity School in Deerfield, Illinois, and then for three years American religion as part of the history of Christianity program at Vanderbilt University in Nashville, Tennessee. Maggie Packer, who had become my wife in December 1969, was a faithful companion as well as an active fellow worshiper at the various churches that supported us along the way. The birth of our first child, Mary, in December 1973, provided a sharp external prompt to wrap up formal education. Throughout these years, my attention as a student was fixed on the Western Christian tradition, particularly Protestants from the Reformation forward. It was also a time when my church identification migrated from generic evangelicalism to the conservative Presbyterianism I was learning about through Maggie, wider reading, and broadening academic networks. Apart from very occasional missionary intrusions, my interests, past and present, remained almost completely Western. The most urgent challenge was how to transfer the purpose I had found in sixteenth-century gospel insights into the day-to-day humdrum of the late twentieth century. The contrasts between that then and our now were, of course, extensive, but I had little desire to explore other contrasts of potentially equal significance between Western and non-Western Christian developments.

At each stage of these academic wanderings I was blessed with outstanding teachers. Because they were outstanding in different ways, it would require a long detour to recognize properly the full roster of those who stick in my memory as particularly helpful. Yet in retrospect I can see that among the most memorable were several who, like Martin Luther though on a smaller scale, took me into foreign places. Those journeys were only in my head, but they were journeys nonetheless. Their teaching gave me the opportunity to look back on my own circumstances as if from afar. The teachers were cross-cultural guides. I was situated, as comfortably as a student could probably be, in a very American present, but through their efforts I was learning a great deal about past times and past peoples who challenged instinctive assumptions, opened new angles for assessing crucial life questions, and in other ways showed what it meant for people and communities to do things differently. Although the explorations in comparative assessment came from Western religious and intellectual developments, they nonetheless prepared the way for later explorations across space as well as time.

In preparing this book, I have been able to dig out several short essays I wrote at various times about some of these teachers. The chance to reread what was written in some cases almost forty years ago makes it easier to see how these guides set me on a path that ended in "world Christianity," though without any realization that I was headed in that direction. Those pieces have also provided useful rough drafts for some of what follows.[1]

---

1. "Remembering Arthur F. Holmes (1924–2011)," *EerdWord* (blog), October 17, 2011, http://eerdword.wordpress.com/tag/arthur-holmes/; "Opening a Wardrobe: Clyde Kilby (1902–1986)," *Reformed Journal*, December 1986, 6–7; "David Wells: The Stability of Grace," *Christian Century*, February 7, 1990, 126–27; "Catching Up With 'The Evangelicals'" [on George Marsden], *Christianity Today*, December 5, 1975, 18–21.

❖

At Wheaton College I remember four professors who were particularly effective in nurturing cross-cultural awareness, two known widely (Arthur Holmes and Clyde Kilby) and two whose good work had greatest impact closer to home (Frank Bellinger and Robert Warburton).

Arthur Holmes, professor of philosophy, was one of the three great intellectual influences at Wheaton over the last half of the twentieth century. The other two exerted their influence from afar—Billy Graham by guiding Wheaton from fearful fundamentalism to evangelistic ecumenicity; and C. S. Lewis through the example of wit, learning, and narrative turned to orthodox Christian ends.

After service in the RAF, Arthur had come to Wheaton on the recommendation of a Baptist pastor in his native Dover, England. In 1951 he began teaching courses in the Bible department but then added philosophy classes as he went on to doctoral studies in that subject at Northwestern University. It took more than a decade and a half, along with a special exercise of the patience for which he was legendary, but Arthur finally convinced the college to establish a philosophy department in its own right. Very early on he also began an annual philosophy conference that enlisted Reformed, Catholic, secular, and a broad range of evangelical philosophers in wide-ranging debates, discussions, networking, and the best kind of respectful controversy.

In 1966–67, I enrolled in Professor Holmes's ever-memorable, two-semester course on the history of philosophy. Holmes was mostly interested in relating the thought of individual philosophers to those who had gone before or came afterwards (rather than, as historians are inclined to do, against the contextual circumstances of the philosophers' own times). Yet the reading was edifying, the tests were a bracing intellectual challenge, and the lectures were luminous. He would wax discursive, keeping eye contact with all and sundry, pause occasionally to lean forward and with a grin ask, "You see, you see?," finesse any questions the illuminati in the class dared to ask, and then move on. He was, as I heard him explain to faculty committees on which I later served, teaching both students and his subject, and doing so superbly. The class remains, in my nonphilosophical mind, a model for how higher education should work.

For the first semester research assignment, I wrote a paper on some aspect of the thought of Clement of Alexandria. I was proud of myself for plowing through the densely packed pages of Clement in the *Ante-Nicene Fathers*, churning out some high-sounding prose about what I'd been reading, and then garnishing it with a little poem I fancied had something to do with the topic. Arthur's laconic response was deflating in the best way: "You should think about publishing this, the poem I mean."

As an author, he produced several widely read books on philosophical topics with Eerdmans, InterVarsity, and other Christian presses. Whatever their particular subjects, they all fulfilled a dual function: urging sectarian evangelicals to consider hard thinking as Christian service and urging the worldly wise to take "Christian higher education" seriously.

Arthur's landmark contribution to evangelical students of my generation was to demonstrate that formal study of philosophy could advance rather than threaten Christian faith. For the path that later led me to world Christianity, his special contribution came in a book published a few years after I took his class, *Faith Seeks Understanding: A Christian Approach to Knowledge* (Eerdmans, 1971). It was the first attempt I can remember that set out a self-consciously Christian understanding of "perspective" as an interpretive category fully compatible with main Christian teachings and yet also able to acknowledge the importance of a thinker's location for all epistemological issues. As a historian who benefited from things like this spelled out in big letters, Arthur's arguments marked out a path for thinking about historical study as informed by integral Christian categories. It was also a prompt toward recognizing a fundamental principle of world Christian awareness: all ecclesiastical, theological, and moral categories are situated (that is, all have a history of indigenization in particular times, places, and circumstances); but all may also participate fully in authentic Christian faith.

❖

Immanuel Kant once testified that he had been shaken awake from dogmatic slumbers by David Hume. For me it was Clyde Kilby at Wheaton College who performed this function. In my case, however, slumber was not metaphorical but actual. In the fall of 1965 I found myself in Kilby's course on the English Romantic poets. The class convened at a postprandial hour, probably 1:00 p.m. or so. For most of the term I was consumed by a passion to play more and better basketball; carbohydrate-laden cafeteria fare lay heavily in the stomach; a stuffy classroom led time after time to the same soporific result. Eyes drooped, body slumped, and the mind drifted away.

Through the mists, however, something extraordinary was getting through. Kilby loved literature, he believed in the imagination, and he could quote Wordsworth with abandon. Most of all he was driven by a passion to disabuse Wheaton fundamentalists of the notion that poetry was a frill, an extra for nailing down the final point of a sermon. Poetry, proclaimed Kilby, was life. And not only life but Christian life. Through my personal fog it started to make sense. I was coming to realize that Christianity was truly important. I knew I liked poems. But I had never before associated the two.

Often in his desultory ramble through the Romantic poets, Kilby would pause to tell us what "C. S. Lewis, his friends called him Jack," had written about this or that. I had no idea who C. S. Lewis was, but Kilby was not going to let any of us escape from his college without finding out.

Kilby, as it turned out, was not just an inspiring teacher but also a determined promoter of Lewis and the circle of British writers in which Lewis moved. At Wheaton, Kilby's efforts to gather material on Lewis eventually blossomed into a formal collection that some years later became the Marion E. Wade Center, an archive and research library devoted to Lewis, J. R. R. Tolkien, and several others either in Lewis's circle or who had influenced him in special ways.

Kilby's efforts to promote the work of these British authors made him, perhaps unwittingly, a force transforming the character of American evangelicalism. His own books about Lewis, his efforts on behalf of the Wade Center, and his encouragement to read these

writers played a major role in popularizing Lewis among fundamentalists and evangelicals, and to some extent the American population
at large.

That effort, in turn, was big with implications for evangelicals at
Wheaton and elsewhere. Was it really possible to receive a clearer, more
forceful, and more winsome picture of Christianity from a British
academic than from the safely didactic pens of American evangelicals?
Was it possible that something really important could be learned from
a high-church Anglican who promoted the work of Roman Catholics,
a literary scholar whose confidence in the Bible did not include the
standard fundamentalist formulas? A perplexed Bob Jones Jr. is once
reported to have said after visiting Lewis: "That man smokes a pipe,
and that man drinks liquor—but I do believe he is a Christian!" Others
of the same background, if not quite the same disposition, were led
to deeper understanding through Lewis's guidance. Thanks to Clyde
Kilby, I was one of them. Again, permanent insight from crossing a
cultural boundary was the enduring result.

At Wheaton College I took a couple of courses in state and local
politics from Frank Bellinger; for one of the classes the main text
was a long book by V. O. Key, either his *Politics, Parties, and Pressure
Groups* or perhaps *Southern Politics in State and Nation*. I forget
the details for why I enrolled in these classes, though knowing that
Frank was the scorekeeper at Wheaton College basketball games,
and so responsible for recording my own very modest contributions
to the team's efforts, may have played a role. More important was
Frank's reputation as an effective teacher of subjects in which I was
keenly interested.

He taught in a low-key, conversational style, quite unlike the pol-
ished declamations of Art Holmes or the wound-up enthusiasm of
Clyde Kilby. Highpoints of the class came when Frank talked about
his own service with the DuPage County Board. I'm sure he was a
Republican, since that party was as dominant in this collar county
(one of the suburban counties surrounding Chicago) as the Demo-
crats were in Chicago. But he was also known as a moderate more

interested in making county government work than in scoring partisan points. (Hard as it may be to imagine now, numerous public servants in both parties at that time approached politics in this frame of mind.)

The long-lasting effect of Bellinger's teaching came from the entirely matter-of-fact way in which he took for granted his own participation, as a Christian believer, in electoral politics. V. O. Key wrote about American political history as a clash of interests; Bellinger said the same and simply moved on. He had positioned himself between what has been for evangelicals a rock and a hard place. On the one side, evangelicals during my early years looked on politics with considerable uneasiness. It was a worldly domain, or at least "second best" to full-time Christian service. My corner of the evangelical world knew of only one US congressman (Walter Judd of Minnesota) and only one US senator (Mark Hatfield of Oregon) who had somehow overcome the much-feared temptations of public life to become recognized as "Christian politicians." On the other side, many evangelicals during recent years have joined the ideological scrum that disdains the give-and-take of ordinary political life. Bellinger showed me a better way. He demonstrated that engaging with political culture could be a natural expression of responsible Christian life. For an evangelical of my generation, this was a gift.

❖

A related gift came from Robert Warburton of the Wheaton College English department, especially in his course on Victorian prose and poetry. For broader personal reasons, Bob remains a much treasured friend and mentor. Besides his duties as a literature professor, he also coordinated the college Sunday school class at Bethel Presbyterian Church that I attended during my junior and senior years. That informal gathering was in many ways more important than my regular classes. It provided an excuse allowing me to cross paths with Maggie Packer; it also showed by example how biblical faith could speak to the broadest possible concerns of human existence. It demonstrated how much the book of Job and Archibald MacLeish's play *J.B.* could illuminate each other.

In his Victorian literature course Bob's teaching was a revelation for the seriousness with which he engaged the assigned texts. For him, there were no easy, pat responses to what the poets and novelists wrote. With Christina Rossetti and similar Christian authors, he probed structure and questioned content with as much healthy skepticism as he brought to Matthew Arnold, Edmund Gosse, and other post-Christians. I retain a vivid memory of how respectfully he tried to draw a not-always-receptive class into Algernon Swinburne's "Hymn to Proserpine," with its haunting opening lines: "Thou hast conquered, O pale Galilean, / The world has grown grey from thy breath."

Later, Bob would oversee the senior thesis I wrote on the novels of Thomas Hardy. That effort showed me that I could write more than one hundred pages and barely scratch the surface of a worthy subject; it told Bob that just because a headstrong student did not always follow his sage advice, there was no reason to stop trying. Even later, Maggie and I were blessed (to use the clichéd evangelical word for which there is sometimes simply no alternative) to enjoy almost three decades as fellow laborers in church with Bob and his wife, Wilma, and then after Wilma's death with Bob and his late-autumn bride, Mary Sheesley.

Through this long and enduring friendship, Bob Warburton's early teaching has continued to instruct: proper understanding requires a willful suspension of preconceived judgments and a determined effort to view things from the other subject's point of view. As a bonus, once the journey to world Christianity described in these pages was well underway, Bob and Mary provided direct encouragement as they reported on their adventures teaching English during several trips to the People's Republic of China.

At the University of Iowa, my time studying comparative literature was probably most important for confirming that I found the historical contexts for literary works more intriguing than any formal or theoretical assessment of their value. These studies also perhaps anticipated my growing general interest in cross-cultural comparisons. By forcing me to work carefully through questions related to translation, the program in Iowa City prepared the way for a broader opening to the world.

The chief push in that direction came in a class on the works of Goethe taught by John A. A. ter Haar. Only decades later did I discover that he was associated with a faculty group that sponsored campus lectures on Christianity and culture. As a student I knew him only as a well-prepared, carefully spoken, and informative expounder of German works that I was struggling to read. Over the course of the semester, it grew somewhat easier to keep up with assignments from Goethe's *Iphigenia auf Tauris*, *Die Wahlverwandschaften*, *Die Leiden des jungen Werther*, and quite a bit of *Faust*—and also to understand more of Professor ter Haar's carefully articulated lectures *auf Deutsch*. But the big payoff was reflection on the constant back-and-forth between German and English. I was reading, hearing, and trying to take notes in the former, but my larger thoughts about Goethe and his work, as well as the paper I wrote that compared plays from Goethe and Shakespeare, were in the latter.

I did not come away with blinding revelation about what happens when words or thoughts move from language to language. (The most manifest lesson of the time concerned Romanticism itself: despite captivating instruction from Kilby at Wheaton and ter Haar in Iowa City, I concluded that the Romantic self was not the model of humanity I wanted to emulate, promote, or spend a lot of time studying.) But from related experiences during my short career in comparative literature, and especially from Professor ter Haar's Goethe class, I came away with not only a deeper understanding of how very complicated the translation process was but also that it was truly possible to communicate at least the substance of meaning from one language to another, and hence from one culture to another. The path opened up to much later instruction concerning the fundamental significance of translation for understanding the character of Christian faith itself.

❖

Two years at Trinity Evangelical Divinity School in north suburban Chicago supplied enough raw experience, at least of the intellectual sort, for a novel or two. (Somewhere around those years I read Martin Gardner's riveting *The Flight of Peter Froom*, a lightly fictionalized account of his experience at the University of Chicago Divinity School. I was much taken with the novel but remained content that my theological education took place at Trinity.) It was a time of vigorous, if precarious, expansion at a school embodying the vision of its dean, Kenneth Kantzer. That vision was for a thoroughly evangelical institution that would remain much closer to historical orthodoxy than Harvard, where he had done his graduate work, while being more ambitious about first-level theological research than Wheaton, where he had taught before coming to Trinity.

As a recently married and vocationally uncertain young adult, but also very much as someone still caught up in a life-transforming experience of divine grace, I was eager to explore the heritage of the church. Trinity's funding was meager, its library holdings eccentric, the enthusiasms of its Jesus people a distraction, and the residual anti-intellectualism of its revivalist heritage an encumbrance. But Kantzer and the capable faculty he recruited were making good on the effort to create an institution both advancing understanding of historical Christianity and speaking to a contemporary fundamentalist-evangelical constituency. At Trinity, it was a time of real excitement. An institution supported by Evangelical Free Church Republicans was spawning an alternative magazine-with-community called *The Post-American* (later, *Sojourners*). The stream of bona fide evangelicals with PhDs from Cambridge, Harvard, and universities only slightly less notable seemed unending. From time to time it was also a place of punctured hubris: the process theologian Schubert Ogden once winsomely tied in knots an admired evangelical scholar at a public debate on issues of revelation and divine authority.

Almost all that was good about Trinity during my time was summed up in the faculty. This talented group was not innocent of overreach, nor were prima donnas unknown. But the good vastly outweighed the bad. Younger students of both Testaments, theologians, and church historians were eager to put serious research to use for the church; they were joined by senior scholars whom Kantzer recruited as permanent faculty or short-term adjuncts.

For me the lights went on most brightly in classes taught by David Wells. From my perspective, he seemed middle-aged and worldly wise, though he could not have been much more than thirty. His Queen's English and academic degrees reflected origins in the south of Africa and study in London and Manchester. But simple intrigue at someone who had come so far to lecture in the Upper Midwest soon passed on to something more substantial in courses on the general history of Christianity and the patristic period. It was what he said, more than the accent in which he said it, that made the difference.

In his lectures, David took for granted the worth of Christian tradition and the compatibility of scholarship and faith. To one who by nurture and nature had found it tortuous to reach such conclusions, the way he simply took these assumptions for granted was a revelation. And then after opening the door, he invited us in to glimpse the beauties of classic Christian doctrine. As he described them, the views of Irenaeus, Augustine, Aquinas, Luther, Calvin, Wesley, Barth, and more shone with a brilliance that my poor faith had never expected to see. We encountered the imperatives of disciplined historical memory (emphasizing the value of trying to see clearly what had been actually thought and experienced rather than reaching for the quick, didactic "lesson"). We perceived the irrelevance of some treasured shibboleths (it was a delicious rumor that David had needed to ask what "premillennial" meant when it came time to sign Trinity's statement of faith). We witnessed the way substantial theology could shape preaching (his sermons were as simple and forceful as many of the ones I regularly heard were facile and unfocused). We were standing alongside him in sharing the delights and perplexities of Christian learning (it remained a much-appreciated lesson in pedagogy that he once asked me about the substance of a late paper and not about its tardiness).

David Wells went on from his days as a Trinity church historian to a distinguished career as a theologian at Gordon-Conwell Theological Seminary. In the intervening decades, my approach to Christian developments has become more contextual, less strictly dogmatic than what he offered so challengingly in lectures and books. Still, I pursue what might be called the social meaning of theology, or the contextual history of Christian doctrines and institutions, and I remain committed to working hard at positioning religious developments against wider political and intellectual environments because of what David taught me at Trinity Seminary long ago: Christian life is rooted in the historical stability of God's grace, and the church's thought takes shape in the culture-embracing character of the incarnation. These verities, absorbed alongside countless eurekas in studying the Christian past, have stood me in very good stead when trying to grasp the shapes of world Christianity.

❖

Several years after my time as a Trinity Seminary student, instruction from David Wells was renewed in an unexpected but entirely propitious way. In 1975, I was hired as an assistant professor of history at the seminary's sister institution, Trinity College. Soon thereafter George Marsden arrived from his regular post in the Calvin College history department for a one-year teaching stint at the seminary. For most of that year, I was privileged to enjoy a weekly coffee hour with George and David, which for me meant much more than any postgraduate fellowship imaginable. In these casual conversations I got to experience firsthand some of the intelligence, godliness, learning, and all-around sagacity that I was simultaneously reading about in the signal characters in the Western history of Christianity—though both George and David displayed a sharper sense of humor than many of the great figures of the past.

Before that year I knew only a little about George, Calvin College, and the Dutch Reformed heritage that Calvin represented. In a couple of undergraduate visits to Calvin's new campus on the outskirts of Grand Rapids, Michigan, I had discovered that students were allowed to smoke at this purportedly Christian college, that some of the professors in those button-downed 1960s sported beards, and that the Knights were unbeatable on their home court. How any of that random information related to Abraham Kuyper, "world and life views," or "the creation mandate" remained secrets to be revealed at a later date.

About George I had come to learn a little through what he had written and through brief but much appreciated personal meetings.

The exact sequence is now hazy, but I believe literary acquaintance came before the face-to-face. In 1975 George contributed a chapter to a book edited by David Wells and his Trinity Seminary colleague John Woodbridge entitled simply *The Evangelicals*. The collection as a whole represented something of a breakthrough since it included essays by several scholars from the academic and ecclesiastical mainline, as well as by a number of evangelicals. Both the evangelical authors, who documented the continuing vitality of evangelical traditions and argued for the maturity of postwar evangelical convictions, and the others, who balanced qualified appreciation with searching questions, presented work of high quality. Marsden's contribution sketching the history of fundamentalists and evangelicals was the best of a very good lot. It outlined with unusual clarity and unusual concision the main stages of fundamentalist-evangelical development from after the Civil War into the 1960s. By likening the lot of religious conservatives in the early twentieth century to that of "uprooted" immigrants deposited in an alien culture, Marsden provided a fruitful analogy for comprehending the reactions of evangelical Protestants to a secularizing America over which they exercised less and less control. Even more impressive was the author's stance: a noteworthy blend of empathy, insight, research, and wit. I think I knew that this essay offered a foretaste of what would become George's *Fundamentalism and American Culture*, published by Oxford University Press in 1980. That book, in turn, cracked open the door to the cascade of serious scholarship on and by evangelicals that has poured forth from university presses since that path-breaking book appeared.

About the same time I was also reading George's 1970 *The Evangelical Mind and the New School Presbyterian Experience: A Case Study of Thought and Theology in Nineteenth-Century America*, a book whose exposition, if not its title, displayed the same insightful concision as his essay on the history of fundamentalism. It too became a light for my path by showing how to join together diligent historical scholarship, empathetic interpretation, and thoughtful criticism when writing about evangelicals in the past. It was especially noticeable that George's prose was as limpid as the best historical writing of his generation. The combination of well-researched information and provocative insight, of evident sympathy with—and compelling criticism of—American evangelical traditions, has remained a model for how I have tried to write about similar American topics, and later for a few topics in the vast domain of "world Christianity."

The icing on this particular cake came from discovering that George, his wife, Lucie, and my wife, Maggie, had all attended—at different age levels—the same summer camp in the Pennsylvania backcountry sponsored by the Orthodox Presbyterian Church. With that kind of serendipity at work, it was no surprise that the Reformed instincts of the person I loved best and the scholar I most admired wore off on me, or that I experienced a great sense of intellectual liberation from coming to absorb some of the Kuyperian instincts that informed academic life at Marsden's Calvin College. (Abraham Kuyper was the obsessively energetic pastor, theologian, newspaper editor, educational reformer, and politician who eventually become prime minister of the Netherlands from 1901 to 1905. His combination of heartfelt piety, bold academic explorations, and conventional European habits [that included smoking, drinking, and allowing beards to grow] exerted a strong influence on the Dutch Americans who supported Calvin College and Seminary, and through those institutions a widening circle of "gentiles" like myself.)

❖

During my years as a student, the character of Christians around the world was being shaped by many developments, but none more important than a fresh engagement with the Holy Spirit. Often (to Western eyes) in unexpected and even disquieting forms, believers throughout the world were experiencing God's presence directly, immediately, and physically. At Wheaton, the University of Iowa, Trinity Evangelical Divinity School, and Vanderbilt University, I was mostly unaware of these momentous developments. Yet through faithful teachers I too was receiving the gifts of the Spirit, mediated rather than unmediated, intellectual rather than corporeal, but genuine nonetheless.

❖ 4 ❖

Settling In

In the mid-1970s the job market for college-level history teachers was constricted, as it has become even more so in the years since. At the time I was intensely gratified to be hired at Trinity College in 1975, after typing up and sending out more than one hundred letters of inquiry during the previous two years and receiving in return only one perfunctory interview and the overture from Trinity. In this new job my main assignments were in American history, though gratitude for the chance to fill any kind of faculty post meant that I was happy to take on other classes when asked, including first and second year German, creative writing, and introduction to American government. Through the good offices of Trinity administrators Edwards Hakes and David Johnston, who were in the business of making sound educational bricks with the straw removed, I was also privileged to teach occasional church history courses at Trinity Seminary (Luther, the Reformation, the Puritans).

The opportunity in 1978–79 to enjoy a year-long seminar at Northwestern University funded by the National Endowment for the Humanities and then in the fall of 1979 to move to Wheaton College appeared likewise as unmerited opportunities. At Northwestern under the direction of Professor Timothy Breen we read classic anthropological texts in order to enrich individual research projects; mine was research into the theological-political-intellectual-educational-ecclesiastical relationships among Presbyterians clustered around Princeton, New Jersey, from the American Revolution through the War of 1812. The position at Wheaton allowed for more concentration on the church history courses for which I had been trained and which remained my greatest interest. While at the time I did sense how unusual the opportunities of an academic career actually were, it was only later that fuller realization dawned concerning the extraordinary gifts of time and intellectual focus they represented. A bookish introvert fascinated by questions about the complex relations between Christian faith and day-to-day life was being paid to read books, carry on research, write my own books and articles, and instruct (mostly) interested students in the complex relations between Christian faith and day-to-day life. These were not gifts that by any stretch of the imagination I deserved. Yet they opened a vocational life that though sometimes harried, occasionally conflicted, always over-scheduled, and once or twice touched by deep disappointment, has been overwhelmingly satisfying. I did not, however, realize at the time how this vocation would itself expand after a decade or so from exclusive focus on Western history to a much wider purview.

❖

At Wheaton I was privileged to function mostly as a "church historian," with a concentration in research on problems of religion in American society. Although I took my turn with Western Civ—and mostly enjoyed the pedagogical challenge of keeping large general education classes reasonably engaged on topics like the Greek philosophers, the Crusades, the industrial revolution, and World War II—most of my courses were electives, advanced classes for majors, or offerings in Wheaton's small MA program in church history. Alongside specialized offerings, the mainstay classes were the history of Christianity in America, Luther and the Reformation, and the history of history-writing. Almost every year I was also responsible for a one-semester general survey of church history from the apostles to the present. Its divisions were conventional: the early church with a concentration on creed, canon, and episcopate; the Middle Ages with special attention to Roman Catholic structures, reform, and theology; the Reformation with Calvin, Zwingli, Anabaptists, Anglicans, and Catholic reformers struggling to elbow Martin Luther aside; and the modern period with a gallop through pietism, the Wesleys, secularization, Kierkegaard, Newman, Lightfoot, Barth, and the Second Vatican Council. Eventually this offering would lead to a new course on the history of Christianity throughout the world, but more or less via a trap door.

Wheaton was in many ways an ideal place for a young scholar who wanted to write but whose intellectual interests were diffuse, with "diffuse" a fancy way of saying "scattershot" or "undisciplined." The college provided some encouragement of its own for publication, it accommodated faculty who sought outside money to support their projects, it maintained an excellent library for subjects in the history of modern Protestant Christianity, and it could arrange dedicated space in the library for faculty engaged in longer-term efforts (hidden away with no phone and no name on the door!). Yet as also a liberal arts college concentrating on its teaching mission, the requirements for tenure and promotion were relaxed enough to encourage faculty writing for general audiences as well as the scholarly guild.

This environment meant that a wide scope existed for publishing with popular Christian magazines, journals sponsored by evangelical institutions, and publishers serving Christian constituencies, as well as for professional journals and university presses. As it happened, many of the Christian periodicals and publishers also maintained high academic standards, or were moving rapidly in that direction. By and large, they expected as much by way of clear argument, careful documentation, and efficient prose as did publishers anywhere; the main difference remained that writers could take for granted a Christian angle of vision.

In my case, as someone for whom writing was always satisfying, if never exactly easy, it was a welcome challenge to be sending out manuscripts and rewarding in return to get back at least some acceptances. The resulting publication record might have merited tenure at a reputable research university, but only if the probationary period for strictly academic work could have been extended to two or three times the normal length. Yet a desultory approach to publishing allowed for a most enjoyable engagement with a fairly broad range of subjects. It has been humbling to notice, if also slightly disconcerting as a sign of advancing age, that the list of my early interests includes several topics about which I am still trying to write something cogent, now four decades on.

The most noteworthy thing about the quick summary that follows now seems to be the entire absence of subjects related to the history of Christianity outside the Western world. From one angle, the summary might seem to display an ambitious range of interests. But from the angle offered by what Christian adherence had actually become by even the mid-twentieth century, it testifies to a thoroughly parochial range.

This early writing included articles and eventually books on topics related to my Vanderbilt dissertation, which examined theology, church order, and politics for New Englanders from the Great Awakening to the Revolution; later came further articles and books from research focused on the early history of the College of New Jersey at Princeton and Princeton Theological Seminary. Based on that same research, some pieces (aimed at more-general audiences) tried to explain why I considered certain political-religious-national actions either edifying or destructive. These publications set a course for what continues as my main academic assignment: teaching and writing about religion in American political and intellectual contexts.

Yet Wheaton also offered enough free space to sustain earlier interests in the Reformation, with some writing on Luther, John Calvin, the English Reformation, and Melchior Hoffman (the subject of my master's thesis at Trinity Seminary). Miscellaneous efforts on the early history of evangelicalism (George Whitefield, Jonathan Edwards, John and Charles Wesley, Francis Asbury) overlapped substantially with my research in American subjects. Ample opportunities also existed for journalism, sometimes disguised as history, on more recent evangelical personalities (J. Gresham Machen, Francis Schaeffer, Frank Schaeffer) and on contemporary problems. There was also time for some writing on general interests like science and Christianity, historical contexts for interpreting the Bible, the broader history of Scripture in America, and the rapidly shifting relations between Catholics and Protestants. The ever-fascinating career of Abraham Lincoln was one of the topics that remains of great interest to this day.

Some years ago a psychologist friend asked semi-innocently, "Why another book?" It was startling not to have a good answer, except that writing is just what I do. A pious response could have pointed out that the vast majority of my articles, reviews, and books have come in response to requests for copy. But that observation begs the question. Whatever the underlying reasons, the urge to figure things out with pen and paper (later keyboard and screen) meant that when I did become interested in Christianity around the world, the chance to write about these new interests provided a helpful way to explore, discover, and begin to analyze.

❖

Two enterprises played especially important roles in my early attempts as an author. Both, in retrospect, helped build bridges to the broader historical interests that came later.

The first was the *Reformed Journal*, a periodical published by the William B. Eerdmans Company from 1951 to 1990. This monthly began as an effort by young and restless Dutch Americans, most associated with Calvin College or Calvin Theological Seminary, to season the traditional theological fixations of their Reformed tradition with broader cultural awareness. The magazine was funded by accounting legerdemain at Eerdmans' highest levels, the editors worked on the magazine by moonlight, its pages sometimes rehearsed quite a bit of inside Dutch baseball, authors contributed for free, and circulation never strayed far above three thousand. Yet right from the start the *Reformed Journal* contributed a refreshing note to American religious journalism. At first concentrating on the denominational affairs of the Christian Reformed Church and educational debates at Calvin, but then broadening out to wider assessment of issues at the intersection of Christianity and society in general, the magazine demonstrated that Kuyperians could speak American. In a famous speech from 1880 that opened the Free University of Amsterdam, Abraham Kuyper had made an extraordinary claim: "There is not a square inch in the whole domain of our human existence over which Christ, who is sovereign over *all*, does not cry: 'Mine!'"[1] By showing that Christian believers had something meaningful to say (or to dispute among themselves) about war and peace, social inequalities, gender reform, film, politics national and international, the experience of cancer, business ethics, Billy Graham and Martin Scorsese, novels, reprobation and supralapsarianism, television, and much more, the *Reformed Journal* worked at fulfilling Kuyper's bold assertion. The magazine was a lighthouse in an often dreary American landscape.

In 2011, Calvin College stalwarts Jim Bratt and Ron Wells published a retrospective collection from the magazine to celebrate the centennial of the Eerdmans Publishing Company.[2] The book testifies eloquently to the *Journal*'s extraordinary reach and to the seriousness of even its whimsy ("these were, after all, Calvinists," as the editors explained in their introduction). But the collection also illustrated the unexpected truth that earnest Calvinists could write as well as anyone.

After reading the *Journal* for several years, I submitted an essay for publication in 1981. Then through George Marsden's mediation I was asked to serve on the editorial committee, a rare honor for someone who had not done duty at Calvin. In the magazine's last decade, it was a privilege to contribute something like forty-five articles, reviews, poems, and personal essays (the latter for the "As We See It" columns at the front of each issue). It was even a greater privilege to attend occasional editorial meetings, either at Eerdmans' own facility or at one of several Grand Rapids eateries whose personnel seemed on unusually familiar terms with the *Reformed Journal* regulars. Serious discussion dominated these meetings, often with matters of world-historic import on the table, but almost always lightened with what from an outsider's viewpoint could only be called eccentricities.

1. "Sphere Sovereignty," in *Abraham Kuyper: A Centennial Reader*, ed. and trans. James D. Bratt (Grand Rapids: Eerdmans, 1998), 488.

2. James D. Bratt and Ronald A. Wells, *The Best of* The Reformed Journal (Grand Rapids: Eerdmans, 2011).

One of the latter moments has a permanent place in *Journal* lore, as recorded by editor-in-chief Jon Pott: "The younger generation had its own stories to add—of, for example, the time [one of the original editors] was asked by one of the newer editors, in the service of a more enlightened etiquette, not to light up a cigarette after lunch, causing much silent consternation in a founder for whom the *Journal*, at least of cherished memory, practically *was* smoke."[3]

The opening to world Christianity that the *Reformed Journal* provided for me once again concerned cross-cultural communication. As had been the case earlier with Martin Luther, C. S. Lewis, and then Goethe, I was learning from the inside about a hitherto unexplored world. In this case it was a fully formed Christian tradition that not only replicated some of what I had experienced but also opened much that was new. Some of the new, like the ability to talk about infinitely important matters with a light touch, represented a simple challenge to broaden my own approach. Even more, a new appreciation of culture, politics, society, and art as God-given venues to explore as a natural expression of Christian life prepared the way for later efforts to understand much different expressions of Christian life taking shape in cultural, political, social, and artistic venues much further removed from my ordinary round than Grand Rapids was from Wheaton. When authors in the *Journal* wrote about South Africa, Hungary, Vietnam, or the Netherlands, the limited range of my experience was being stretched. How they wrote about such places, and many more things beside, stretched me even further.

❖

The second enterprise that played an important role in my early attempts as an author was the Institute for the Study of American Evangelicals (ISAE), created at Wheaton College in the early 1980s. Like the *Reformed Journal*, it became a window to a wider world. The ISAE represented the confluence of a number of forces. It gave form to a casual network of younger historians from evangelical backgrounds who shared interests researching historical aspects of Protestant life in

3. Jon Pott, "Publisher's Note," in ibid., xvi.

North America. The institute required the willingness of Wheaton to house programs that pushed the college toward hitherto unexplored efforts in research, collaboration, and publication. The institute was made possible by the philanthropic generosity of the Lilly Endowment and the Pew Charitable Trusts, funding agencies that chose to direct some of their means to self-identified evangelical projects. And it took advantage of new interest among academic historians in the religious dynamics of the American past.

In November 1979, Wheaton College sponsored a conference on "The Bible in America," some of whose presentations became a book of the same title published by Oxford University Press in 1982 with contributions from Harry Stout, George Marsden, Timothy Weber, Grant Wacker, Richard Mouw, Gerald Fogarty, Nathan Hatch, and me. Hatch, then a young professor at the University of Notre Dame, had secured funding from the Lilly Endowment for this effort, and I arranged for Wheaton's sponsorship through the college's new Billy Graham Center. The conference attracted a lively audience, with at least modest interest in the book that followed. Its publication had been eased by the recent success at Oxford University Press of George Marsden's *Fundamentalism and American Culture* and by the fact that George contributed one of the key essays to *The Bible in America*. From that beginning point, funding came from Lilly to establish a center at Wheaton to study other aspects of American religious history, with special concentration on the contributions of evangelicals. Under the leadership of first Joel Carpenter, then Larry Eskridge, Darryl Hart, and Edith Blumhofer, the ISAE went on to sponsor over thirty separate projects, most of them involving public conferences and published books. Major funding continued to come from Lilly and Pew, with Wheaton providing continuity and overhead. Topics ranged widely, from Jonathan Edwards and evangelical mass media to the history of theological education, women in twentieth-century Protestantism, and a general account of American religious history.

Some of the participants in ISAE projects are featured in later chapters in this book for their special contributions that pointed toward world Christianity. Here it is important to record that the networking of scholars convened by the ISAE represented a kind of graduate level education without the mechanism of a graduate school. Even more particularly, it eventually became evident that serious study of evangelical and evangelical-like forms of Christianity did not have a natural stopping place at American borders. Raising eyes to take in Britain did not seem like a stretch. But in the early days of the ISAE no one was thinking about Canada, much less the rest of the world. Yet once the ISAE set out to make the study of evangelical history a serious enterprise, it was not long until the study could not be contained within the nontrivial but still artificial boundaries of American national experience.

In the late 1970s and 1980s, however, neither my taking part in the work of the *Reformed Journal* nor my enjoyment of the satisfying beginning of the ISAE seemed obviously related to more than deeper investigation of American experiences. It was not quite true that my axis mundi ran only from Wheaton to Grand Rapids, but almost. Soon, because of developments taking place in a constricted space that was as limited intellectually as it was geographically, things were about to change.

❖ 5 ❖

Moving Out I

In the early 1980s I thought I knew with reasonable certainty who I was and where I was headed. Marriage and family were the center of daily existence but sometimes in ironic competition with my aspirations as a scholar-teacher. I knew it was absurd to think that, if only I could concentrate all energies on producing works of Christian scholarship, that would set an ideal life course. The idea that "Christian" might also mean something about how to treat one's nearest and dearest, about considering colleagues and students as more than learning machines, about responsible participation in a Christian congregation where fellow members could not care less about the *American Historical Review*, or about how the children of God might contribute to the peace of cities in which the Lord had placed them—such bare-minimum insights at least partially restrained heedless academic ambition. For the sake of practicing authentic Christian life, instead of just reading about it, Maggie and I had resolved as much as possible to keep the Sabbath—despite what lectures, deadlines, or strategic meetings were on for Monday. This effort certainly helped to keep the necessary reminder fresh that scholars should be humans too.

Apart from the challenges of sanctification, I thought that I was set. Ongoing experience of the goodness of God's grace in Jesus

Christ was a foundation requiring no alteration. I was entirely content with the range of American-centered historical projects that made up my intellectual purview. While some aspects of the evangelical milieu in which I found myself were disquieting, that milieu, when considered in the round, seemed as good as any Christian alternative and certainly acceptable as a fruitful context for family, work, and worship. I remained convinced that the classical Protestantism of the Reformation provided a solid foundation for faith and works. That conviction received periodic secondhand support from reading books that were as bracing for how they modeled the historian's craft as they were convincing in the history they recounted (Roland Bainton, Gordon Rupp, Philip Watson on Luther; A. G. Dickens on the English Reformation; John T. McNeill on the history and character of Calvinism; Jaroslav Pelikan, who gently contextualized sixteenth-century insights into the entire sweep of Western Christian tradition). The same conviction also received firsthand reinforcement from some of the conservative Presbyterians in our immediate acquaintance and even more through the Reformed variant absorbed from the Calvin College Kuyperians.

Academics too easily substitute bibliography for biography, but fresh reading was building steadily on these foundations. I valued John Stott's *The Cross of Christ* as an up-to-date, evangelically inflected refresher on Martin Luther's most fundamental theological insight. Multiple oral interpretations of *The Lord of the Rings*, an exercise that began with our oldest child around 1979 and continued for almost two decades, confirmed deep in my subconscious the power of narrative. Without necessarily finding a completely satisfying account for Christian approaches to historical study, it was still encouraging to read what E. Harris Harbison and Herbert Butterfield had to say on the subject. About supposed conflicts between science and Christianity, it was a great boon to read landmark histories by James R. Moore and David Livingstone, and then to have multiple occasions actually to talk about such matters with these two distinguished scholar-friends. Boyd Hilton and Quentin Skinner expanded on the insight I had first learned from Arthur Holmes as they showed in detailed historical works how all formal discourse, including theology, was embedded in the circumstances of its own time and place—whatever the transhistorical value of such discourse might be. Dorothy L. Sayers, by precept and example, added Anglican support to Kuyperian testimony concerning the sanctity of daily work done wholeheartedly as unto God.

These propitious influences lay in the background as I continued to research problems in American history. It took a long time to finish the book that appeared in 1989 as *Princeton and the Republic, 1768–1822: The Search for a Christian Enlightenment in the Era of Samuel Stanhope Smith*. But despite delays, it proved rewarding to continue the effort begun at Northwestern under Tim Breen to figure out how the American Revolution, philosophical conflict, institutional crises, personality clashes, theological debates, and the spread of democratic ideology affected the broad circle of Presbyterians who supported the college at Princeton, and from 1812 the seminary as well. Quite a while before that book appeared I was gathering material for a broader project on how these same factors interacted to shape American theological development more generally from the time of the colonial Great Awakening to the period of the Civil War. That book also took a long time in coming, finally published in 2002 as *America's God: From Jonathan Edwards to Abraham Lincoln*. Yet for all the new information uncovered by research for these books and for all the effort it took to narrate cohesively how individuals and larger forces interacted, those books mostly remained within a trajectory begun with a paper on Charles G. Finney that I wrote for Professor John Gerstner at Trinity Seminary and mostly interacted with standard (and exceedingly helpful) books in American history. For academic purposes, in other words, I was more than content to be an "American historian."

❖

Some years ago I was asked to contribute to the latest round of the *Christian Century*'s perennially interesting "How My Mind Has Changed" series. Without that encouragement, I'm not sure I would have seen how things began to shift for me throughout roughly my fifth decade (1986–96). This chapter outlines what that shift entailed, but with one exception. The exception is the basis for the rest of this book, which explains my latter-day avocation geared to understanding something about the shape and meaning of Christianity as a global reality.

In turn, because of the self-reflection required for this memoir, I think I can see how the general developments of that earlier period prepared the way for real interest in Christianity outside the Western world. But I'm not sure. So let me first try to explain the general picture—assisted by material prepared for the *Christian Century*—and then attempt an explanation for how I think these matters relate to the later concerns of this book.[1]

Change in understanding the ways of God in the world, and in understanding myself, took place amid circumstances where God manifested himself more viscerally, through both absence and presence, partially in disciplined study, but even more directly in life circumstances. As only a partial list, the circumstances included a wrenching church split, the death of my father who in his latter years had become a very good friend, the death of a very good friend who had become like a father, and the confusing pain of other friends' dashed hopes. In these situations—where "answers" were scarce—the Christian faith remained no less real. In fact, it became more intensely real.

One way of describing that intensifying reality is to speak in general terms. For what were probably personal reasons, but also reflected certain conventions of postwar American evangelicalism, I had once thought of Christian life as the arena where hard-won principles were "applied," where a proper grasp of the faith was put to work in realizing the faith in practice. Without giving up that notion entirely, I was coming to feel that the relation between conviction and experience was much tighter, much more interdependent than I had once thought.

1. The following paragraphs make use of much that first appeared as "Deep and Wide: How My Mind Has Changed," *Christian Century*, June 1, 2010, 30–34, and then reprinted in *How My Mind Has Changed*, ed. David Heim (Eugene, OR: Cascade, 2012), 53–64.

The change went from thinking about the truthfulness of classical Christianity, the beauty of its breathtaking drama, and the effort
of Christian living as relatively discrete matters—to experiencing
Christian truth, Christian beauty, and Christian life as a whole. Put
differently: the change went from thinking that I needed to work hard
at bringing together the believer's general vocation in Christ and
my specific calling in the academy to realizing that my task was to
discover already-existing organic harmonies. Again, from conceiving
the boundaries of "genuine" Christian faith narrowly to thinking that
these boundaries might be capacious in ways I had hardly imagined.

Another way of describing the journey of those years is to focus on
what might be called theological aesthetics, and then, more concretely,
on Christian reality deepening through believing friends who stood
alongside during dark days, through hymns sung and recalled, and
through the celebration of the Lord's Supper.

As the years have passed, the basic dogmas of the Nicene Creed
have become more important; they now seem truer than in the hour
I first believed. From that hour I knew that Christianity was deep and
that it was beautiful. In the years under consideration here I was coming to believe the depth was unfathomable and the beauty supernal
beyond telling. I also was coming to believe that no single word could
describe the faith, though "dogma," "story," and "reality" all caught
something of what was confessed in saying that almighty God made
"the heaven and earth"; that "the only Son of God . . . true God from
true God" was the one "through [whom] all things were made"; that
this one "for us and for our salvation . . . came down from heaven"
and was "incarnate from the Virgin Mary"; and that he was "for our
sake" crucified, died, was buried, and rose from the dead on the third
day; and that his "kingdom will have no end" as it is extended forever
and ever by "the Holy Spirit, the Lord, the giver of life."

The deeper and wider ramifications of Nicene Christianity are difficult for me to disentangle because it has been through experiencing
their unfathomable depths that the surpassing breadth of classical
Christian faith has grown clearer as well. The changes represented

an incremental growth in awareness over the years rather than illumination through striking eurekas. The experiences prompting these changes have been various, their effects cumulative, and their influence overlapping.

"Fellowship" was the in-group word for what took on new force during those years. This standing together through duress seemed simple but was anything but. It was the "communion of the saints," not as the result or the product of what came before these words in the Apostles' Creed, but as an instantiation of those realities. First and always most important was communion in Christ with my spouse, then with a wide circle of friends, fellow church members, and associates at work. Our pastor in those years was a pastor indeed, a shepherd who certainly did some herding, but more importantly stood with, prayed with, and wept with the sheep. I had had such a pastor once before, but not until these later years did I realize how much the empathic gentleness of that shepherd of my youth had done to maintain an opening for faith.

Hymns did not exactly take on new meaning; rather, I began to sense more clearly why the best had been so consistently moving since at least the early-adult years of self-conscious faith. Regarded simply as texts, they could offer unusually evocative communications of strong theology. But their gripping force lay in the affect—not simply words alone, but the more-than-rational conviction they communicated through the combination of careful writing and compelling music. It could not have been a coincidence that in those years J. S. Bach became, as he has been for so many others, a kind of fifth evangelist. Sometime in this period I was also delighted to discover that Charles Hodge, the nineteenth-century lion of Princeton Seminary, who has been so often criticized for writing theology as an exercise in scientific biblical rationalism, suggested on several occasions that hymns and devotional writings from the far reaches of the church could construct an entirely sufficient account of the Christian faith.

A significant bonus in thinking about why the best hymns worked so powerfully at cognitive, emotional, and spiritual levels lay in recognizing where these particularly gripping hymns came from. As

basically a Calvinist myself, I nonetheless saw immediately that the
best hymns came from many points on the Christian compass. Some
were ancient (e.g., Ambrose of Milan, "O Splendor of God's Glory
Bright"), some were contemporary (e.g., Margaret Clarkson, "For
Your Gift of God the Spirit" ["He, who in creation's dawning brooded
on the lifeless deep, still across our nature's darkness moves to wake
our souls from sleep"]). Some were heavy (e.g., Johann Heermann,
"Ah, Holy Jesus, How Hast Thou Offended" ["I it was denied thee:
I crucified thee"]), some were light (e.g., Fanny Crosby, "Rescue the
Perishing" ["Jesus is merciful, Jesus will save"]). They came not only
from fellow Calvinists (e.g., the Strasburg Psalter's "I Greet Thee Who
My Sure Redeemer Art"), but also from the winsomely zany Count
von Zinzendorf ("Jesus, Thy Blood and Righteousness"), from Men-
nonites, Disciples of Christ, Catholics, Pentecostals, independents,
and especially from the implacably Arminian Charles Wesley (e.g.,
"Arise, My Soul, Arise" ["Arise, my soul, arise, shake off thy guilty
fears, the bleeding Sacrifice in my behalf appears. . . . my name is
written on his hands"]).

Such effective hymns went deep because they communicated the
core dogmas of the Nicene Creed with unusual force. Concentration
on those core dogmas made them singable by believers almost everywhere; the singing turned instruction into love.

The experience that prompted the deepest reflection on the nature
of Christianity and my own life as a Christian was regular celebration
of the Lord's Supper. For years our Presbyterian church in the western suburbs of Chicago celebrated Communion in the Scots' Form
where congregants came to the front, sat at tables, and were served
the elements by our elders. This experience in retro-Calvinism conveyed conviction beyond words—in part because it was an intensely
communal experience (we knew the joys and sorrows of many who
moved forward to communicate) and in part because it was always
accompanied by music (we sang good hymns, some old and some new,
that focused on the work of Christ "for us and for our salvation").

What drew this cyclone of emotion into sharpest focus was when
the elder—almost always a man or woman whom we knew and

respected—spoke our names in giving out the elements and then said, "This is the body of Christ broken for you," and "This is the blood of Christ shed for you," or similar words. (A poem I wrote sometime in the early 1980s tried to capture some of what was going on.)

Scots' Form in the Suburbs

The sedentary Presbyterians
awoke, arose, and filed to tables spread
with white, to humble bits that showed how God
almighty had decided to embrace
humanity, and why these clean, well-fed,
well-dressed suburbanites might need his grace.

The pious cruel, the petty gossipers
and callous climbers on the make, the wives
with icy tongues and husbands with their hearts
of stone, the ones who battle drink and do
not always win, the power lawyers mute
before this awful bar of mercy, boys
uncertain of themselves and girls not sure
of where they fit, the poor and rich hemmed in
alike by cash, physicians waiting to
be healed, two women side by side—the one
with unrequited longing for a child,
the other terrified by signs within
of life, the saintly weary weary in
pursuit of good, the academics (soft
and cosseted) who posture over words,
the travelers coming home from chasing wealth
or power or wantonness, the mothers choked
by dual duties, parents nearly crushed
by children died or lost, and some
with cancer-ridden bodies, some with spikes
of pain in chest or back or knee or mind
or heart. They come, O Christ, they come to you.

They came, they sat, they listened to the words,
"for you my body broken." Then they ate
and turned away—the spent unspent, the dead

recalled, a hint of color on the psychic
cheek—from tables groaning under weight
of tiny cups and little crumbs of bread.

Many years before, it had been intellectually thrilling to read Martin
Luther as he expounded on the *pro me, pro nobis* (for me, for us) of
the gospel. Over the years, the intellectual frisson became an exis-
tential epiphany. I am not convinced that anyone has fully captured
the dogmatic details; none of the classic formulas that have tried to
explain "the real presence" of Christ in the Lord's Supper are entirely
satisfying. But whether in Orthodox, Catholic, Lutheran, or Calvinist
form, I became convinced that in the Eucharist God draws participants
into the fellowship of his Son. If I was ready, if I was not, if my sins
lay heavy on my soul, if I had a momentary difficulty remembering
recent transgressions, if there were distractions, if attention was perfectly focused—the circumstances were far, far less important than
the phrases ending with "for you," than the eating and the drinking.

Reflection on the force of what transpired so regularly drove me
to the following conclusions. The Lord Supper encompasses life so
powerfully only because it speaks of events that really happened and
dramatizes dogmas that mean exactly what they say. But being invited
to share in the rite and enjoying the privileges of believing the dogma
requires a transforming experience of the whole person. It pushes
vigorously against pretense, ego, pride, self-serving, irony, and all the
other postures that come so easily to all humans, maybe especially
to the intellectually attuned. It enacts emptiness being filled, guilt
overcome by grace, strife restored to communion. It demands my
soul, my life, my all.

Brad Gregory's magnificent history of persecution in the Reformation era, *Salvation at Stake*, offers an especially compelling account
of Eucharistic realities.[2] In that strife-torn period, it was most often
differences over what the sacrament meant that made Europeans will-
ing to die—and kill—for their faith. Western civilization has certainly

---

2. Brad S. Gregory, *Salvation at Stake: Christian Martyrdom in Early Modern
Europe* (Cambridge, MA: Harvard University Press, 1999).

progressed since the sixteenth century in abandoning capital punishment as a means to adjudicate conflicts over the Lord's Supper, but it has also suffered a great loss. That loss is retreat from our ancestors' knowledge that life and death are at issue in every offering of the wine and bread with the words ". . . for you."

Another book that I read years later, Peter Thuesen's compelling history of the doctrine of predestination throughout American history, offered academic confirmation for some of what I was thinking. One of this book's main conclusions, and in my opinion one of the shrewdest possible reflections on the whole history of Christianity, focused on the means by which humans apprehend divine revelation. The book argues persuasively that the key theological division in Western Christian history has not been between defenders of divine sovereignty and proponents of human free will but between Christian communities keen to *define* the divine-human relationship and Christian communities marked more by sacramental practice than by precise doctrines. In Thuesen's words, "There are two larger ways of being religious—two forms of piety, two religious aesthetics—that have existed in tension in Christian history. . . . In place of predestinarianism's mystical awe before God's electing decree, sacramentalism cultivates mystical wonder before the power of priestly ritual."[3]

Through the fellowship of Christian community, through the ongoing encouragement of hymn singing, through regular participation in the Lord's Supper—through, more generally, a stronger organic understanding of life, work, meaning, God, others, and self—I was undergoing not so much a dramatic change as a deepening apprehension of my place in the gospel story. During those same years my interest was growing in Christian developments beyond—in some cases, far beyond—the American present and the American past. Now being constrained to write about those parallel developments, I see them connected in the following ways.

❖

3. Peter J. Thuesen, *Predestination: The American Career of a Contentious Doctrine* (New York: Oxford University Press, 2009), 6–7.

My growing sense that the key affirmations of the Nicene Creed described absolutely fundamental reality had a curious effect on how I was coming to think about Christian doctrine more generally. Through this process, dogma was actually becoming more important, but the range of dogmatic questions that now seemed of first importance shrank considerably. That God in the gracious mystery of trinitarian mercy reached out to unworthy sinners was granite bedrock. How exactly? With what parsing of actions between divine selection and human response? Through which roles played by church, parents, self, tradition, and the Holy Spirit? Such questions remain more than merely intriguing, but no longer of life or death importance. Similarly, while the divine origin and superintendence of nature was now a given, figuring out how creation and providence actually worked became a less pressing concern. I was more and more convinced that the Bible told the story of salvation as perfectly as could be imagined, but less and less concerned to resolve the difficulties involved in stating how the Living Word was fully revealed in the written word.

I knew that alternative answers to these and other doctrinal questions, as presented by the various Christian traditions, were significant. But perhaps from a historian's instinct, it was becoming at least equally compelling to learn how the particulars of the various Christian traditions represented cogent answers to particular questions in particular times and places. I was fully assured that "Jesus is the answer," but increasingly convinced that the questions prompting this definite response varied over a wide range of possibilities.

To reason this way opened the doorway wide to the world history of Christianity. It was, for example, a short step from being captivated by the effort to understand why "tradition" became such a threatening word to American believers in the wake of the American Revolution to being captivated by why Chinese Christians in the seventeenth century found it so natural *as believers* to continue honoring their ancestors. Once entering on such a path, the road stretched invitingly ahead.

It was the same with Christian community. If I was finding out—existentially—how deep and strong the bonds of Christian fellowship were, shouldn't I expect to find—as an observer—the same depth and strength of Christian community in other times and places? Even if those conditions followed norms far different from my own? If my pastor, in imitation of the Good Shepherd, ministered so effectively to me, shouldn't I expect to find the same Shepherd ministering just as effectively through other pastors in every imaginable circumstance? If the Good Shepherd was the One in whom God loved *the world*, how could it be otherwise?

Hymn singing led in similar directions.[4] Most obvious was the simple ecumenicity of the Western hymn tradition. If that ecumenicity anticipated the songs from every tongue, nation, tribe, and people referred to in the book of Revelation, it certainly had to extend beyond just Western musical traditions.

That reflection pushed further toward a consideration of culture as embodied in musical styles, conventions, and practices. It was clear that the dogmas of the enduring hymns were universal. But it was also clear that the music that played such a powerful part in quickening the dogma was particular. Isaac Watts's "When I Survey the Wondrous Cross" remained fairly inert on the page without an effective tune such as "Rockingham" by Edward Miller or "Hamburg" by Lowell Mason. I might find singing this hymn with a rock-and-roll melody or accompanied by a five-toned Thai xylophone an intellectual curiosity but it would not be heartfelt worship. Over time the obvious became clear: the hymns did their great work for me as they were sung with music originating from only about two hundred years of Western musical history (1650–1850). With music not from the West and with later or earlier Western music, the affect was simply not the same.

Extension was the next step: If I was experiencing the universal gospel through a particular cultural expression, it followed that the same gospel could be as powerfully communicated through other cultural expressions, even if those expressions were alien or foreign to me. The experience of those who could be moved by a rock-and-roll rendition of "When I Survey the Wondrous Cross," or by a five-toned

4. The following paragraphs are modified from "Praise the Lord: Song, Culture, Divine Bounty, and Issues of Harmonization," *Books & Culture*, November/December 2007, 14–15.

Thai version of a similar hymn, was, in principle, just as authentic as when I sang these words to "Rockingham." Understood in this way, the hymns were making me at the same time both eager to explore other cultural expressions of the faith and more convinced about the fundamental truths that hymns could communicate.

Again, as the depth of experiencing the Lord's Supper opened up, it did not take long to intimate also how wide the experience had to be. If it was true that God reached out to me through the celebration of Communion, so it was true that he reached out to all who took part in the rite. I continue to believe that differences in how the celebration takes place—differences in theology, authority, practice, belief, and more—are far from insignificant. Yet it strikes me as still more significant that all who are called to the table are opened to experiencing the grace for which it stands and which it communicates. With considerable arrogance, I even believe that this account of God acting toward us in the sacrament holds true for fellow believers who regard it as only symbolic and even—through yet another mystery—for those few believers who do without Communion entirely.

Another poetic effort, this one written somewhat later, tried to communicate those universal implications. That poem was probably too ambitious, since it was written to the somewhat unusual meter of William Fullerton's "I Cannot Tell," a hymn that our congregation sometimes sang during Communion.

Somewhere Every Day

[11 10 11 10 D]
From South and East, from West and North they gather,
on foot, by car, in rickshaw, tram, and bus,
in health, in wheel chair, in joy, in sorrow,
relaxed, uptight, disheveled, and fastidious.
They come, O Christ, to you, to taste the body
that once for all was slain, to sing and pray
and take a cup whose balm brings life from dying—
throughout the world and somewhere, somewhere every day.

The words they hear when they have come together
are chanted, lisped, intoned, or simply said

and tell in myriad tongues with every accent
of body broken and of life's blood shed.
Mere words convey a gift of perfect freedom,
a debt of love that no one can repay,
a yoke of new and welcomed obligation—
throughout the world and somewhere, somewhere every day.

The spaces where they meet are huge, resplendent,
or huts and hovels all but falling down,
on Sundays jammed but often solitary,
both nowhere and on squares of world renown.
Yet all are hewn from just one Rock unbroken
in whose protection no one is betrayed,
which lets itself be smashed to bits for sinners—
throughout the world and somewhere, somewhere every day.

The hands that tender host and cup are youthful,
emaciated, worn, and manicured.
They take so little time, they bring so little,
to do a work by which so much is cured.
These hands that bring the Savior near are icons
of hands once torn in order to display
with lines of blood the names who come receiving—
throughout the world and somewhere, somewhere every day.

❖

The preceding paragraphs may describe connections that were not nearly as definite as they now seem. But at least from this autobiographical distance, they do help explain how shifting life circumstances prompted broadening historical interests.

In any event, I am sure that two life-altering events really did take place about the time when this broader shift was getting underway. In the summer of 1984 I met George Rawlyk, and in June 1986 I heard a lecture from Andrew Walls.

❖ 6 ❖

Looking North: A Guide

George Rawlyk was a good historian, he combined enough size (six and a half feet, maybe 240 pounds) and athletic ability to be the fourth overall pick in the Canadian Football League's draft for 1957, he was unashamedly Slavic, he was a Rhodes Scholar, and he was very much a Canadian. In countless gatherings over the decade I knew him, George would invariably tell the group how things looked in "a Canadian context." What *exactly* such a context entailed might not have been crystal clear, except that he was convinced about the importance of *difference*: North America did not reflect a single historical trajectory and whatever "American culture" meant it did not speak univocally for Canadians.

Getting to know George took place about the same time that the process described in the previous chapter was under way. He was the most important personal stimulus for another new venture during that same period, which was my growing interest in Canadian history. Granted, it was a small step from concentrating on history in the United States, but a step nonetheless. George was the gatekeeper; beyond lay the True North Strong and Free, as the English version of the Canadian national anthem puts it. And beyond Canada? For me, it was the world.

❖

George Rawlyk's parents were Ukrainian—his father immigrated to Canada and his mother was born in Canada. They lived in Thorold, Ontario, on the Niagara Peninsula.[1] George's father, who worked in a paper mill that supplied newsprint to American publishers, bequeathed to his son an identification with working people as well as considerable suspicion of international corporate power. The household language for George and his two older sisters was Ukrainian. Rawlyk's primary early influence from outside the home, including first steps in English, came through a mission conducted in his neighborhood by a single woman, Mary Renton, for the Baptist Convention of Ontario and Quebec. Almost as early, he took part in club activities organized for youth by the Communist Party. When he was in the tenth grade he had what he later told his sisters was a "spiritual experience" at a weekend sponsored by the Inter-School Christian Fellowship. Thereafter he worked with Mary Renton in the mission and soon joined a Baptist church. During his time as an undergraduate at McMaster University, and despite a full athletic and academic schedule, he returned home on weekends to help at Mary Renton's mission.

George remained an active member of local Baptist churches for the rest of his life. He was also frequently a sponsor of Christian student organizations on campus (except for a period when he was asked to step down as sponsor of the local InterVarsity group at Mount Allison University in New Brunswick because of his support for the National Association for the Advancement of Colored People). As a lifelong democratic socialist, he was a firm supporter of Canada's left-wing alternative to the Liberals and Conservatives, the New Democratic Party.

In 1957 Rawlyk received a bachelor's degree in history from Mc-Master University, where he was also a standout center on the football team. The next two years he studied in Oxford as a Rhodes Scholar and then returned to North America for graduate work in Canadian

1. A great deal of biographical information can be found in *Revivals, Baptists, and George Rawlyk*, ed. Daniel C. Goodwin, Baptist Heritage in Atlantic Canada 17 (Wolfville, Nova Scotia: Acadia Divinity College, 2000), 29–51.

history at the University of Rochester. He taught at Mount Allison and then Dalhousie University in Nova Scotia before moving in 1963 to the history department of Queen's University in Ontario. He would later chair the department during a tumultuous decade of rapid expansion and ideological conflict in Ontario higher education. That service as department chair was ending just as he made contact with what he feared were fundamentalists from south of the border.

Rawlyk first made his mark as a historian of the eighteenth century, particularly of relations between New England and the Maritime colonies of Nova Scotia and New Brunswick. Much of his scholarship, early and late, dealt with the meteoric career of Henry Alline, a passionate revivalist whose electric preaching promoted a "New Light stir" in that region for several years before and after Alline's early death in 1784. As someone who had been studying the place of religion in the American Revolution from early in graduate school days, I was particularly intrigued to learn from George that Alline's powerful itinerant preaching helped keep Nova Scotians fixed on local concerns and therefore unresponsive to New Englanders' invitation to join the American Revolution. The elements that made Alline endlessly fascinating to Rawlyk were the revivalist's populist style, his intense preoccupation with spirituality, and his ardent commitment to the lives of ordinary men and women joined together in deep congregational fellowship.

It was not, however, until Rawlyk reached the midpoint of his career in the early 1980s that he discovered academic guidance for how he could write about Alline (and religion more generally) in terms respecting both the integrity of spiritual experience and the conventions of academic history. These insights included accounts of cultural hegemony from the Marxist theorist Antonio Gramsci and the liminality of religious communities from the anthropologist Victor Turner. Most important was the example of other North American historians who were beginning to publish academic works on evangelical groups, of which George Marsden's *Fundamentalism and American Culture* was always of first importance.

Rawlyk then produced a torrent of writing, especially on Canadian radical evangelicalism in the late eighteenth and early nineteenth centuries as influenced by Henry Alline or those who extended his message. That particular interest soon led to more expansive publications on Canadian religious history generally. Those books included a path-setting edited volume on the history of Protestants in Canada from the takeover by the British (1760) to the recent past and a landmark historical examination of evangelicals in Canada. The latter volume came from a splendid conference Rawlyk organized in the spring of 1995, which drew interested participants from Ireland, Italy, Scotland, England, and Australia, as well as from the United States and throughout Canada. With characteristic energy he had secured revisions for the thirty-four papers going into that volume, and also drafted the book's introduction, before his untimely death in November of that year.

In his latter years Rawlyk was also cooperating with the public opinion researcher Angus Reid to write on religion in contemporary Canada, especially about signs of evangelical commitment found not only among conservative Protestant groups but also among mainline Protestants and Roman Catholics. Along with his edited colloquy on the history of Canadian evangelicals, that book—*"Is Jesus Your Personal Saviour?" In Search of Canadian Evangelicalism in the 1990s*—was published posthumously. Throughout his latter decades, Rawlyk insisted on the irreducible integrity of Christian experience. He also refused to equate the apparent health of churches, almost all of which had declined steadily in Canada, with residual religious interest.

As in much of his strictly historical work, Rawlyk's assessment of contemporary Canadian religion featured a strong sense of distance from the United States. In fact, "anti-American" would not be too strong to describe the preface he penned for this last book, which was written while Rawlyk was on leave (during the winter) in the American South, and very much offended by the political preaching he heard in Baptist churches he visited. (As a side note: "penned" was in his case literal; George never learned to type, a possible defect that he turned into a campaign on behalf of low-wage workers by arguing that the Queen's history department could not lay off members of

its secretarial pool so long as a full complement of able typists was
required to transform his scrawl into something legible.)

❖

My introduction to George occurred at the Craigville Conference
Center on Cape Cod in the summer of 1984. Under the leadership
of Joel Carpenter, Wheaton's Institute for the Study of American
Evangelicals (ISAE) had secured enough grant money to convene a
short summer colloquium for planning projects and sharing works in
progress. George had been reading books by George Marsden, Nathan
Hatch, Harry Stout, and a few others in the loose ISAE network.
He was especially intrigued that Marsden had been able to write
empathetically, but also critically, about the history of fundamentalism. Yet as a Canadian nationalist, a democratic socialist, a critic of
American involvement in the Vietnam War, and someone very suspi-
cious of capitalist Big Business (including the enterprises that funded
the ISAE), he was also wary. A few personal contacts encouraged him
to think that meeting these American fundamentalists might not be
a complete disaster. They included two historian friends with whom
he had cooperated in writing the history of Loyalists who ended
up in Canada after the American Revolution and in researching the
back-country New England revivalists who had been influenced by
Henry Alline. A Queen's University history major who had gone on
to study for a master's degree at Wheaton also piqued his interest.
Thus, when Joel Carpenter extended an invitation to the Craigville
gathering, George accepted.

Joel reports that when he picked up George at the airport, this very
large Canadian sat huddled in a corner of the backseat, nervously
assessing his fellow passengers and wondering if he was being spir-
ited away into the clutches of a Right-Wing Conspiracy. Very soon,
however, the ice thawed—or in a more appropriate metaphor, the ice
firmed up and George was skating along merrily with the Americans,
inept at hockey though we were. Shared historical interests helped,
but even more was resonance with the Americans' critical engagement
with evangelical history and contemporary evangelicalism. Perhaps
most important was the rapport George created with the spouses

and children of the historians. It had been possible for the grants to reimburse expenses for families to attend these summer meetings; their attendance had always served to moderate at least some of the blinkered academic fixations of the historians. With George's presence, this element immediately became more important. He loved kids, kids loved him, and he warmed to the challenge of including wives (and an occasional husband, since most of the historians were men) in the circle of fellowship. (Early on he also cooperated in the need to differentiate given names by accepting "Big George" for himself and contributing to several variations on "Little George" for the intellectual leader of our pack.)

Over the years, George's role in pointing this group of historians toward human, and not just simply academic, interests grew steadily. Joel Carpenter, as part of his remarks at George's memorial service that was held at Queen's in January 1996, explained one of the secular liturgies by which George carried out that function.

> Did George ever tell you about the annual softball game we played on those retreats? He was the full-time pitcher for both teams, and the umpire as well. His job, as he saw it, was to enforce equity and to temper the competitive spirit. The resulting game we called "Canadian socialist softball." With George as arbiter, every kid got a hit, junior professors who were too aggressive on the base paths were called out, and every game ended in a tie. Whenever the score became tied in the late innings, George would look up at the sky and say, "I see rain coming," or "It's getting too dark." Then he would roar, "Game is called; it ends in a tie!" Nothing worked better to nurture the communal spirit of the ISAE than this annual ritual.

Through an association lasting only slightly more than a decade, George helped edit two books from ISAE projects, contributed essays to four others, and became an indispensable mainstay as advisor and friend to many historians in the broader ISAE network. Largely through those friendships, he broadened our historical perception. George could write about high ecclesiastical politics, but he much preferred research on the lives of ordinary believers. He was greatly interested in Canada's national politics but insisted that a marginal region like the Maritimes deserved to be treated as seriously as the center. At least by the time he made contact with the ISAE circle, he was not embarrassed to write about revivalists and to be called an evangelical, yet he insisted that "evangelical" be defined as broadly and as ecumenically as possible. He was, in other words, pushing scholarship closer to life and life closer to scholarship.

In addition, and particularly significant for me and one or two others, George was our first personal link to the wider worlds of Canadian history.

During his tenure at Queen's, Rawlyk inspired not only fear but also reverence as a demanding teacher. Six weeks before his death, George was awarded the degree of doctor of civil law, *honoris causa*, from Acadia University in Nova Scotia. Part of the presentation for the degree from one of his former students, Professor Barry Moody, spoke of that teaching:

> For more than thirty years, he has stimulated, provoked, bullied, encouraged, terrified and *taught* several generations of young historians. His seminars were the stuff of which legends are made, to which students frequently went in fear and trembling, but also in great anticipation, for this was a big man, both physically and intellectually. If one survived the first grueling months, one eventually discovered that beneath this gruff exterior was a compassionate, caring individual, to whom his students meant a very great deal, whose careers he followed closely after they left his seminar nest, and for whom no effort or exertion was too great.

As a research mentor, he supervised more than 120 theses and dissertations on a wide range of topics in Canadian political, social, and religious history. As teacher and mentor at Queen's, as the editor of an influential series in religious history from the McGill-Queen's University Press, and through many acts of extraordinary personal kindness to students and friends, Rawlyk exerted a singular influence both on scholarship about evangelicals in Canada and as a Christian scholar himself. He died on November 23, 1995, from complications arising from an automobile accident two weeks earlier.

❖

After George's untimely death, I wrote the following poem. It was undoubtedly too cryptic—naming break-away Quebec nationalism as "the Yugoslav" disease, referring obliquely to his father's employment, and not pausing to explain the "squeezerinos" or all-encompassing bear hugs that he bestowed on children. But it did express a sense of loss that was partly historical and Canadian, but mostly personal.

Big George

O Canada,
can you survive without George
Alexander Rawlyk there to fight the Northern creep
of Yankee signals, sects, and selves?
Can any take his place to give the Yugoslav disease
its name? Will any still recall what dogged muscle
from Ukraine—with naught in hand, and *then* the crash—
once pulled with steady will from gritty mill?
Who stands on guard for you?

O George,
Rocky Mountain of the North,
you were so craggy and so unexpected.
Slavophile ecumenicist, peasant intellectual,
Baptist socialist, terrifying teddy bear,
a Genghis Khan to start September seminars
become by May a Father Brown.
Why now? For us, whose hearts were just
as poised to crack as Canada?

O Jesus,
ravisher but also knitter up
of hearts, stir up our hope for Canada
the Good, receive our gratitude for this
Melchizedek, and in your mercy let
us pass along his squeezerino, please.

O Canada. O George. O Jesus.

George Marsden's comment after the funeral, which he, Nathan Hatch, and I attended with our wives on a sleety Ontario day, was even more perceptive. During the fall of 1992, Rawlyk had spent a delightful sabbatical at Notre Dame, where Marsden and Hatch taught and during which time he grew even closer to their families. Nathan and George were spontaneously struck by the same biblical images for what our friend had meant to the Americans who, against the drift of over two hundred years of North American history, had been pulled more and more into his Canadian orbit:

> Nat then said exactly what I was thinking of saying. That was that George seemed a sort of Melchizedek to us. In terms of our American and Reformed categories he seemed to walk into our lives from outside our own worlds. He also appeared, especially in retrospect, as a sort of Christlike figure, showing us what it ought to mean for academics to follow Jesus. We just did not expect Jesus to be quite so large. Of course, George realized like the rest of us that he was flawed and, as his minister said [at the funeral], only a sinner saved by God's grace. This is reassuring too for those of us who aren't very good at imitating either the type or the antitype.

❖ 7 ❖

Looking North: Insight

So how did friendship with George Rawlyk, and through that friendship a growing interest in Canadian history, open a door toward world Christianity? Part of the answer was George's own example. He took the history of missionary work seriously, including sponsoring several graduate students who wrote theses on Canadian missionaries. He also maintained an active membership at Kingston's First Baptist Church where he supported the missionaries this church sent out as well as the church's program aiding refugees fleeing from Central America and Cambodia. George's own immigrant roots also sensitized him to how experiences from far away could come to bear on Canadian life.

In addition, George was a strong supporter of efforts by the Institute for the Study of American Evangelicals to broaden the scope of its projects beyond merely the United States. Through these projects he met younger scholars from Australia, South Africa, and other faraway places. In characteristic fashion, he then went out of his way to encourage them in their own historical labors, but he also brought that work into conversation with historical studies about North American topics. In 1993, he traveled all the way to Australia in order to take part in a conference organized by the Center for the Study of Australian

Christianity, but mostly to lend whatever encouragement was possible through his personal presence.

As my bridge to broader engagement with Christian history throughout the world, Canada itself soon became more important than even this memorable Canadian friend. That impetus grew not only from the sheer fascination of discovering fresh information about the Canadian past but also from realizing how useful that fresh information was for most interesting comparisons with American history and, even more, for hinting at larger realities about Christianity itself.

❖

For a historian concentrating on connections between religion and politics in the American past, Canada's history proved immediately compelling. Quite a few things in the two histories were the same, but much was different, and different in most intriguing ways. The paragraphs that follow reprise earlier attempts that I have made to describe those differences.[1]

Canada and the United States are both representative democracies. Both are heirs to the time-tested legal, political, and cultural traditions of Britain but also beneficiaries of strong immigrant streams from the European continent, Asia, and other parts of the world. Both were deeply committed to the Allied side in the twentieth century's great world wars, and both stood solidly with the West during the Cold War (though with Canada not as actively engaged in this latter struggle as the United States).

Parallels between the two nations' religious histories include similarly active Protestants who in the nineteenth century (outside of Quebec) came close to establishing an informal Protestant establishment. Canadians once also joined Americans in using biblical images to describe their nation. Again, like the United States, Canada suffered

---

1. "Canadian Counterpoint," in *Religion and American Politics: From the Colonial Period to the Present*, 2nd ed., ed. Mark A. Noll and Luke E. Harlow (New York: Oxford University Press, 2007), 423–40; "Canada," in *The Encyclopedia of Politics and Religion*, 2nd ed., ed. Robert Wuthnow (Washington, DC: Congressional Quarterly Books, 2007), 1:95–99; and "What Happened to Christian Canada?," *Church History* 75 (June 2006): 245–73. All of these include considerable documentation.

from a dismal record of Protestant-Catholic violence in the nineteenth century. Canada has sustained an active revival tradition, indeed, sometimes sharing itinerant evangelicals with the United States. In both nations, the Catholic Church and mainline Protestant bodies have acted with proprietary concerns to guide the broader society. In both, a variety of liberal-conservative disagreements have divided the churches (although with proportionately more of those divisions in the United States than in Canada). And in both countries there has been ample room for non-Christian religions to flourish. In sum, an awful lot of parallel history—even shared history—joins the United States and Canada. But that shared history makes the contrasts, especially as they affect religion and political life, all the more illuminating.

A number of commentators have traced the most important national differences to geography and history. Canada's vast space and sparse population have required a more active government and placed a premium on cooperation. Historically, the first decision was the most important. In the 1770s Canadians rejected the American Revolution. This rejection meant that Canadians would follow a less republican course, meaning considerably less fear of large concentrations of power. This course was fixed in both Quebec—where Catholic bishops and people remained loyal to Britain during the Revolution despite American diplomacy and invasion—and in the Maritimes and Upper Canada (Ontario)—where many Protestant Loyalists fled after being ejected from their former homes in the new United States. Then, in the War of 1812, when the outnumbered Canadians, with some help from Britain, fended off several American invasions, the result was not only a solidification of Canadian loyalty to Britain but also a significant reduction of cultural influences from the United States, including church influences.

Canada's own republican revolutions in 1837 and 1838, which occurred as separate efforts in Quebec and English Canada, fizzled almost completely. The formal disestablishment of Canada's churches took place in the wake of these failed rebellions. Yet in Canada, disestablishment did not lead to runaway religious pluralism, as in the United States, but to the informal authority of two religious monopolies. For

Quebec, with a fully functioning state-church system, and the rest of Canada, where Anglicans, Presbyterians, and even Methodists had hoped to re-create church-state systems similar to what they had known in Britain, it meant adjustment to denominational difference rather than the all-out denominational competition that prevailed in the United States. Put differently, Catholics in Quebec and Protestants elsewhere retained more features of European Christendom than survived in the United States.

The American Civil War frightened Canadians, most of whom abhorred slavery but also feared the North's mobilized military might. Reaction to that war was a prime factor hastening creation in 1867 of the Dominion of Canada. This new Dominion emerged as a free and democratic nation managed by its own responsible government under the imperial oversight of the British Parliament—in other words, what the thirteen colonies might eventually have become by way of peaceful evolution had not the violent American Revolution intervened. Significantly, the founding motto of the new Dominion was simply "peace, order, and good government," which announced a less ambitious political goal than the Americans' "life, liberty, and the pursuit of happiness."

Again, a contrast is important. American independence took place in the 1770s as a reaction against centralized government; with the exception of the Civil War period, Americans refused to grant much power to central federal authorities until the Great Depression, World War II, and the civil rights movement precipitated a large increase in the scope of the central government. In Canada, by contrast, Quebec began as a society trusting the centralized leadership of the church, and then of business and governmental leaders in league with the church, while English Canada long had a similar corporatist character. More recently, however, American power has flowed to the central government, while Canadian power has moved toward the provinces.

Social indicators also underscore American-Canadian differences: Canada's far lower murder rate, its much-lower number of police per capita, its willingness to tolerate higher taxes, its enforcement of nationwide gun control, its general contentment with relatively high levels of governmental regulation, its single-payer health systems (funded in significant part by the federal government but administered by the provinces), and from 2005 its relatively calm acceptance of same-sex marriage that was legislated by the national Parliament.

A foremost explanation for these national contrasts is to remember the ongoing presence in Canada of two separate societies of relatively equal political weight (French and Catholic, English and Protestant) united in a single nation. Both the United States and Canada have been free, democratic, and capitalist. But, comparatively speaking, Canada has been more organic, traditional, statist, and hierarchical, while the United States has been more free, democratic, local, and individualistic.

In the broad sweep of history, Canadians used forces of cohesion to bind a widely scattered people—indeed, two peoples—into a prosperous, well-ordered, and reasonably stable nation-state. Religious faith and practice were critical in building this nation-state. In the United States, active religion also contributed materially to the construction of American society, but here it was mostly through forms of Christianity expressed in voluntary and individualistic terms. The United States has been more at home with the operations of a free market than Canada, where voluntary exertions have always been balanced by a reliance on government, and where free-market initiative has been matched by respect for received authority and inherited traditions.

Other distinctives setting Canada apart from practices in the United States include stricter enforcement of Sunday closing laws and much stricter restrictions on independent religious broadcasters. By contrast, the religious views of major political leaders have usually been subject to much less public scrutiny than has been customary in the United States. Only in recent years have Canadian media reported on the religious lives of candidates, but not nearly to the extent common in the United States.

One of the most important reasons for structural differences in religion and politics between the two nations comes from the varied proportions of active religious participation. Reports of church attendance offer a particularly significant comparison. After World War II, when the Gallup Poll first asked Canadians whether they had been in church or synagogue sometime during the previous seven days, a full 67 percent of Canadians responded positively. Among all Canadian

Catholics, the number was a robust 83 percent and in Quebec a strato-
spheric 90 percent. In the early 1960s, weekly mass attendance in the
rapidly growing cities of Montreal and Quebec remained quite high,
but some leaders worried openly that in working-class neighborhoods
it was down to "only" 50 percent. By 1990, positive response to the
Gallup question had fallen to 23 percent throughout Canada. Some
observers have noticed a slight uptick in these numbers recently, but
they still hover at 20 percent or lower.

Numbers, of course, must be interpreted, but these findings indicate
a series of shifts in Canadian religion that have not taken place in the
United States, or have taken place at a much slower speed. Put generally,
in 1950 Canadian church attendance as a proportion of the total population exceeded church attendance in the United States by one-third to
one-half, and church attendance in Quebec may have been the highest
in the world. Today church attendance in the United States is probably
one-half to two-thirds greater than in Canada, and attendance in Quebec
is the lowest of any state or province in North America. Over the course
of only half a century, these figures represent a dramatic inversion—and
they raise any number of provocative questions of interpretation.

With official government promotion, Canada has increasingly af-
firmed the value of a multicultural society, a process that in the United
States has moved in the same direction but through different means.
Since the 1960s, Canadian self-identification has shifted massively
from what it once had been—language (English or French) plus religion (Protestant or Catholic)—to new markers. For Quebec, those
markers still include language but are now in league with nationalist
sentiment rather than religion. Cultural heritage is also very important,
especially for secular Francophones in Quebec, but also for Chinese-
Canadians and other newer ethnic communities. Regional identification remains strong for many in the Maritimes and Western Canada.
Lifestyle choices are increasingly significant, especially in the great
urban centers of Montreal, Ottawa-Gatineau, Toronto-Hamilton,
Calgary, Edmonton, and Vancouver (which account for almost half of
the nation's entire population). And as in the United States, economic
status provides powerful identity for large numbers.

For Quebec the change has meant defining provincial identity in cultural and nationalistic terms instead of religious terms. In the rest of Canada, historic markers of Christian civilization seemed to give way almost as rapidly, if not with the same shock as felt in Quebec's once overwhelmingly Catholic society. As was visible at the celebration of Canada's centennial in 1967 and with Expo 67 at Montreal's World Fair that same year, public symbols and rhetoric moved away from particulars of Canada's British history (including British religious history) and toward a vision of universal multicultural toleration.

Under Prime Minister Pierre Elliott Trudeau, Canada "patriated" its constitution and promulgated a new Charter of Rights and Freedom. These developments reinforced the move of Canadian society in American directions. In typical British fashion, Canada's "constitution" had long resided only in the decisions of Britain's Parliament that created the Dominion and regulated its place in the Commonwealth, along with the traditions of English common law. After much labor by Trudeau and many others, the British Parliament in 1982 formally handed over all Canadian authority to Canada itself. Significantly, this action also involved the promulgation of a Charter of Rights and Freedoms that was intended, like the much shorter American Bill of Rights, to guarantee not only personal liberties but also, in Canada's case, the liberties of the provinces over against Ottawa. Unlike the American Constitution, the Canadian Charter referred directly to the deity: "Canada is founded upon principles that recognize the supremacy of God and the rule of law." But like the American Bill of Rights, the Canadian Charter has also stimulated great concern for personal liberty and personal choice. The most visible long-term effect of the new Charter has been to push Canadian judges into an increasingly American pattern where activist jurisprudence promotes social change.

This rapid and crude race through Canadian history hopefully indicates how interesting the subject can be for its own sake. Even more, I hope it shows why my new understanding of Canadian history opened highly interesting questions of more general application.

❖

As figuring out Canadian-American differences became even more intriguing, I was being prepared to think about other comparisons in Christian histories far beyond North America. For example, to learn why Canadians have never been as concerned about separating church and state as Americans prepared me for study of recent Christian history in the islands of the Pacific where some Christian communities have set up mini-Christendoms with considerable overlap between public institutions and the churches.

Again, reflecting on the great differences between Canadian and American history, arising from the fact that the United States was once a slave-holding society, led to ripple-effect reflections concerning other parts of the world. On the one hand, understanding the kind of violence that slavery built into American culture has given me more sympathy for recently Christianized regions in, say, Africa, where inherited patterns of violence sometimes continue despite massive church growth. On the other hand, the relative absence of violence in Canadian history, even as Canada has secularized more rapidly than the United States, gives me an angle for thinking about the European countries where church participation has fallen dramatically but where some marks of "Christian civilization" (like the rule of law and low levels of violence) remain. Had I not thought about such comparisons first between the United States and Canada, I might never have considered other comparisons elsewhere.

I would not have been able to describe it in these terms during the 1980s, but the chance to learn a little Canadian history has also helped me think more deeply about the Christian faith itself. This process represented an extension of what I had already begun to learn from Western church history, which was that authentic Christian life could never be strictly equated with the beliefs or the practices that I considered normative for true Christian faith. Thus, unusually effective teachers like Pope Gregory the Great and Thomas Aquinas had modeled exemplary dedication to self-giving pastoral care (Gregory) and God-centered intellectual effort (Thomas)—yet I did not believe what they believed about the exalted virtues of monastic life. Charles Wesley's Arminian theology made little sense against my own Reformed beliefs, but I sang his hymns as superlative guides to joyful sanctification. Søren Kierkegaard seemed plain kooky in many of his actions and some of what he wrote, but he was able to challenge the nominal Christianity of his day far more effectively than ever I had done.

And so from the Western past I now arrived in Canada, which though still in the West had been to me almost completely terra incognita. There I discovered Jean-Olivier Briand, the Catholic bishop of Quebec during the American Revolution. I could not embrace the bishop's Catholicism, but his reasons for remaining loyal to Britain seemed more compelling to me than the reasons advanced by numerous American clergymen for throwing off British rule, even though the theology of those clergymen was closer to my own. I encountered also Tommy Douglas, the Baptist minister and founder of the socialist Cooperative Commonwealth Federation, whose theology was too liberal for me to accept but whose public advocacy on behalf of those least able to care for themselves set him apart as one of the most admirable Christian politicians of the twentieth century—anywhere. From another point of the theological compass, it was a treat to learn about Ernest Manning, a dispensational Bible teacher and advocate of "social credit"—a theological system and an economic/political platform that seemed equally erroneous to me. Yet as a pastor, radio preacher, and longtime premier of Alberta he won nearly universal respect as a person of nonpareil integrity.

❖

The general direction in which Canadian history nudged me was toward a conviction that essential Christianity meant Christian reality embodied in concrete circumstances—but embodied often in quite different ways and in very different circumstances. I did not yet have a theology in which to frame such inchoate thoughts, but exposure to Canada strengthened instincts that had already been moving in that direction. The theology, however, was not long in arriving.

❖ 8 ❖

Moving Out II

Next came Don Church and Romania. I had met Don during my short, undistinguished tenure with the Wheaton College football team in the fall of 1965. He was one of the coaches, and I had been recruited after the first game of the season when several ends went down with injury. Since I had played that position in high school and was not quite cured of fantasies about multiple-sport stardom, I signed up. (My first three weeks on the Wheaton team let me experience as many losses as the Jefferson J-Hawks had endured during my two years on varsity in Cedar Rapids. Nineteen sixty-five was not a good year for Wheaton football.) Don Church's main assignment, though, was as the track coach. In that role sometime in the 1970s he began taking his teams on trips abroad, partly for the extra competition but partly to assist missionaries and local churches. These ventures soon expanded as Don invited Wheaton faculty to accompany the teams and then to venture out on their own. Central America was the first venue, but soon he somehow developed extensive contacts in Czechoslovakia and other Eastern European countries.

In the early 1980s Don's connections reached Romania. Somewhere he had met leaders of the expanding network of Baptist churches in that country who asked if he might assist their efforts in theological education. Romania still labored under the heavy hand of the Communist dictator Nicolae Ceauşescu. His regime allowed for only a bare handful of Baptists to train for the ministry at a tightly monitored seminary in Bucharest, even though the country's hundreds of Baptist churches were clamoring for pastors. Teachers from the West might fill some of the gaps if ersatz arrangements could be made. The scheme that Don worked out with ex-pats in the Chicago area was to send a pair of Wheaton professors into Romania, ostensibly as tourists, where they would be met by local church leaders who arranged short-term seminars for eager members of their congregations. The teaching had to be done quietly since religious activity outside of tightly regulated public worship services was illegal. In the early years of this program, Wheaton teachers would enter a dwelling, lead discussions and classes for two weeks (while not so much as peeping out of doors), and then leave as unobtrusively as possible. Books and other materials for the summer would be gathered in Wheaton, handed over to representatives of the Romanian Missionary Society in the United States, and mysteriously reappear with no questions asked at the seminars in Oradea, Cluj, Iasi, Arad, and other cities with strong Baptist churches.

Don Church's role was always in the background—making contacts, raising money, recruiting faculty, handling details. It was an operation in the classical mode of evangelical mobilization: no hierarchy, few committees, low to nonexistent overhead, lots of personal initiative, and quite a bit made up as he went along. Yet, by all accounts, highly effective. The Romanians reported great appreciation for the instruction and, even more, for practical evidence of concern from the West. The Romanian students were invariably earnest; their number included quite a few very bright autodidacts actively studying the biblical languages, learning English (and sometimes German) in order to read theological books smuggled in from the outside, and exhibiting levels of commitment to theological education rarely found in the United States. If the Wheaton seminars were beneficial for the Romanians, they were life-transforming for the Wheaton faculty. For

us it was a revelation to be working with students who were so eager
and who took such risks to participate.

❖

Recruiting efforts by faculty who had earlier taken up this assignment, along with Don's persistence, led to my participation on two
occasions, July 1989 and July 1991. The timing of these trips could not
have been more propitious for a historian who had long been an avid
reader of books on the European past. The first trip occurred during
the dying days of European communism, the second as the exhila-
rating excitement from throwing off Communist rule began to fade.

In 1989 we were allowed to take in one Bible each but nothing
else that might indicate our purpose for visiting the country. In 1991
the capacity of our suitcases for books and related material was the
only limit. In 1989, although the Baptists were becoming ever bolder
at simply going about their business, the regulatory hand of an oppressive state was palpable everywhere—phones tapped, currency
manipulated, meetings monitored by the *Securitate*, armed soldiers
patrolling, draconian border controls. (This last circumstance led to
the improbable result of Wheaton College supporting the American
tobacco industry since informal protocols recommended a few packs
of cigarettes as a helpful way for placating intrusive border guards.)
In 1991, the Baptist churches still labored under difficulties, but of
a very different kind. Some of the lay students who had so eagerly
attended nightly evening lectures were now too busy at their places
of work; we heard of several who had been promoted to positions of
considerable responsibility because of their reputations for honesty. In
1989 several of the churches we visited featured the singing of native
Romanian "carols" accompanied by ancient brass instruments (like
valveless French horns if memory serves). In 1991 the music often
featured handheld mics, electronic keyboards, and imported gospel
pop sung in English. In 1989 we were told that the border police were
looking particularly for drugs, pornography, and Bibles. In 1991 these
previously banned commodities seemed to be available everywhere.

❖

In 1989 I was accompanied by Jerry Root, a theologian and an expert on the works of C. S. Lewis. As a sign of conditions softening somewhat, Jerry's wife, Claudia, could also come along. As it happened, communications with Wheaton about plans for the summer had been only partially successful—arranging for seminars or lectures always involved messages passing through multiple intermediaries. But our hosts in Oradea were well accustomed to improvising, so our time was well spent.

Jerry and I each lectured seven different times, through a translator, to the "School of the Prophets," a class of lay people and potential pastors who met three or four evenings a week for basic theological training from 5:00 to 9:00 p.m.—throughout the whole year. Thirty or so people attended these lectures. Jerry, who at the time was writing his PhD dissertation on Lewis and the problem of evil, spoke about the importance of philosophical insight for Christian believers, classical arguments for the existence of God, and apologetic strategies against common anti-Christian arguments. My subjects included reasons for studying the history of Christianity and then some of the main events of Western church history. I tried to offer as much as I could (which, sadly, was not much) on the history of Eastern Orthodoxy since Orthodoxy had long been the default religion of the Romanian people.

Because we could not bring notes or other teaching aids with us, I had come with only a few numbers scratched on an index card—70, 325, 381, 451, 800, 1054, 1517, etc.—as an outline indicating important dates in church history. Developing these "turning points" into regular lectures proved successful enough to attempt the same approach for semester-long classes at Wheaton and also for adult education in church; the result several years later was a textbook, *Turning Points: Decisive Moments in the History of Christianity*, now in a third edition from Baker Academic, which would never have seen the light of day without the help of Nicolae Ceauşescu and his attentive border guards.

During the day, Jerry, Claudia, and I each spent a great deal of time with advanced students who had been given general responsibility for preparing then to teach later when the Oradea Baptists might be able to establish full-scale theological education. Jerry spent most of his time with a young man who was already pastoring a church while also working a regular job. My main partner was a physician whose probing questions partly concerned facts of church history, but even more he wanted to know how study of the past might benefit the church in the present. Paramount to him were questions of divine guidance and how believers might see the hand of God in the events of daily life. Jerry's friend was one of the many bright younger Baptists who, after the fall of Ceaușescu, went on to finish a PhD at a British university and become a recognized theologian himself.

Jerry, for whom this was his second trip to Romania, was prepared for what happened when we attended church, but I was not. Because of glitches in communication, there was some preliminary confusion as to who was meeting us, when, and where. Nonetheless, before we had been in Oradea for twenty-four hours, we had both brought "greetings" to perhaps six or seven hundred worshipers at the Sunday evening worship service of the First (or Hungarian) Baptist Church, with "greetings" involving words of friendship and a brief exposition of a scriptural passage, and I had done the same to the roughly three thousand people crammed into the Second (or Romanian) Baptist Church for their evening service. On the next Friday, Jerry preached and I brought greetings at the regular midweek service at Second Baptist (maybe twenty-five hundred in attendance). Then on Sunday Jerry and I preached or greeted smaller congregations at three services in two outlying villages.

The worship services were deeply moving. The singing, from both the congregations and choirs, was intense; the audiences, in some cases hanging from the rafters, attended to the reading of Scripture with rapt attention; even the children paid close heed throughout services that never lasted less than two hours. Before and after these services, we were the center of exceedingly friendly attention—some of it, no doubt, from a desire to try out English and some for the simple novelty of seeing American visitors up close, but some of it was for serious conversation about the ways of God in the world.

Every night after our lectures, we were invited into the private homes or apartments of Second Baptist members, usually individuals who had some kind of position at the church. These evenings, which could go late, involved some jeopardy for our hosts since they were ignoring the law that required Romanians to report all conversations with foreigners. We talked about church and spiritual concerns, but conversations also veered toward the practical (they asked if we could purchase soft drinks at the hard-cash shop for a young mother who was dying of cancer) and the political (they also wondered why dictators clung to a façade of ideology as they blatantly secured their hold on power). Then late at night, through dark, deserted streets, we were driven back to the nearby resort whose hot springs supplied our ostensible reason for being in the country.

On the way back to the United States, I was much relieved to decompress for a couple of days in Switzerland, which included a visit to Constance, where in 1415 a famous church council had condemned Jan Hus, the renowned reformer, to death. The oppression and general poverty that we had witnessed during the previous two weeks in Romania contrasted dramatically with the controlled order that was everywhere so manifest in Switzerland.

For obvious reasons, the Roots and I were fascinated by the high political dramas unfolding throughout the rest of that momentous year. In July 1989, we arrived in Eastern Europe only shortly after the crackdown on demonstrators in Beijing's Tiananmen Square, the Baltic Republics declared their sovereignty, and Solidarity won its first outright victory in Polish elections. When we passed through Budapest on the way to Romania, we saw crowds streaming into a newly opened McDonald's and also observed posters advertising Billy Graham's arrival later that summer. Shortly after we returned to the United States, Hungary opened its borders to visiting East Germans, allowing them to depart without hindrance to the West. In the fall of 1989, prayer meetings for peace in Leipzig drew thousands and then tens of thousands, Mikhail Gorbachev refused to use troops against the protesting East Germans, and the Berlin Wall opened. Democratically elected governments assumed power in Poland, Czechoslovakia, and Hungary. In December 1989, protests in Timisoara, Romania, at the removal of a popular Hungarian Reformed pastor led to large-scale demonstrations, the fall of Ceauşescu, and then the speedy execution of the dictator and his wife.

❖

Two years later in 1991, when I returned to Romania with New Testament scholar Robert Yarbrough, there was a lot less political drama. To be sure, we were concerned that the highways taking us (and our rental car) through Hungary might be clogged with traffic due to ethnic strife in Yugoslavia. But for the most part, the sense of coming to an alien corner of the world was much reduced from that feeling two years before.

In Cluj-Napoca we lectured to three different groups over a two-week span, while being hosted with great kindness by a couple whom Bob had met on a trip the year before. As an indication of how things had changed since my last visit, our host had to leave before our two weeks were up because, as a self-employed sweater maker, his presence was commanded at a conference in Oxford on "the Christian as Businessman." Since a member of the British Parliament had pulled strings in a couple of Eastern European capitals to secure a visa for our host, he felt he should go—it was his first trip out of Romania.

For three days we addressed a group of nonprofessional Christian artists on "Christianity and Culture." Bob used material from both Testaments to talk about biblical understandings of beauty and ugliness, and I offered a survey of church history with special attention to different Christian attitudes toward the arts. Only two or three of those who attended were connected with Protestant churches, with most of the rest Orthodox by background (though some alienated from that communion) and some Roman Catholics as well.

These lectures, and indeed our entire time in Cluj, were complicated when Bob and our rental car were drafted to help in extraordinarily complicated negotiations between a visiting American woman and a Roma family from whom she was trying to adopt a child. This episode involved tough negotiations with the Roma at their homestead some distance from the city, so Bob's willingness to drive when no other car was available played a critical role in moving along a process for which there seemed to be no ground rules whatsoever.

The American, along with the Romanian Baptists who were trying to help her, lacked transportation and other material support, but as a contrast with only a short time before, they were now free to try for the adoption.

Our second set of meetings involved a group of advanced Baptist students with whom Wheaton professors had met in previous summers. This seminar convened all day for most of six different days. Bob lectured on the use of the Old Testament in the New, while I offered a capsule history of Christianity that focused on differences between Eastern and Western forms of the church, the unfolding of the Reformation, and lessons from the history of Pietism for contemporary Baptist efforts. While a number of these Romanians were still in the early stages of their training, others were as sophisticated as any graduate students Bob and I had encountered in the United States. It was a productive seminar, though the Romanians were obviously tired and busy with many more tasks and opportunities than I had witnessed in 1989.

The third meeting came from contacts Bob had made in the previous summer with a small group of Hungarian Reformed students, ministers, and professors. The Hungarian Reformed included a fairly broad range of theological factions, with the group that had invited us representing the more evangelical portion of their church's spectrum. Our general theme was "Calvinism and Culture," with Bob bringing to bear biblical material, while I discussed historical precedents and lessons learned.

This time, on the way back through Switzerland, I had the great privilege (for a Protestant church historian) of attending Sunday worship in Zurich's Grossmünster, the church where more than 450 years before, Ulrich Zwingli's scriptural expositions had sparked the Reformation in Switzerland.

❖

These two Romanian trips took place as I was just being drawn into consideration of "world Christianity" as more than an extension of "Western Christianity." I was beginning to see some of the things that I can spell out now but was not yet taking them all that seriously.

One concerned the great contrast I felt between East and West, as a visceral, bodily sensation, toward the end of the first trip. I had had to bribe the hard bargaining cabbie who took me to the Bucharest airport (he refused to take Romanian currency and insisted on being paid in what was for him illegal American money—I was short of the latter but had somehow reserved an Eisenhower dollar coin that did the trick). At the airport, a pack of Camels, strategically extended, got me past the guard who inspected my luggage and who, thus, paid no attention to the cache of Romanian Baptist publications stored at the bottom of my suitcase. On the way out to our plane, we passed soldiers with Kalashnikovs at the ready. The plane itself was parked far enough out on the tarmac that we could see tanks arranged on the runway margins. When the wheezy flight on Tarom Air finally deposited me in clean, efficient, orderly, law-abiding Switzerland, I felt like kissing the ground.

Two years later it was a moving experience to worship in Zwingli's church, to witness a mother and father bring their infant for baptism (as older children scampered about the nave), to hear an exposition of Romans 8 that would have gone over equally well with Romanian Baptists and Wheaton evangelicals, and to sing several stately hymns accompanied by the Grossmünster's mighty organ (restored since the days when Zwingli had that musical instrument removed because it was not mandated in Scripture). To be sure, attendance at Zurich's Grossmünster numbered far fewer, in that commodious space, than had crammed into the Romanian Baptist churches we visited. But the sheer pleasure—physical, cultural, aesthetic, spiritual—at experiencing the legacies of Europe's Christian civilization very much on display in Zurich, despite the obvious secularization of its population, was intense.

And yet. Were not those Zurich streets once as soaked with the blood of interfaith martyrs as the streets of Timisoara and Bucharest had recently been bloodied with sacrifices to regime change? Had not the Baptists of Romania in less than a century displayed loyalty to Scripture, sanctified self-discipline, and even some culture-building efforts at least on a par with Protestants in the early days of the

Reformation? And were not the bulging Baptist churches of Romania a rebuke to the sparsely attended edifices of Switzerland? Clearly, I was responding to the contrast between Bucharest and Zurich as a tourist, rather than as a real historian. Why was I so stuck on comparisons from only the present when I should have been thinking more about Romania circa 1990 as compared to Switzerland circa 1525?

Then there was a series of reflections about the great differences I had observed between the two visits. These thoughts were pushing outward toward a realization that the embodiment of Christian faith in any time or place always reflected the particular circumstances of that time or place. As the realization grew that the Zurich sermon I heard could also have been preached in Oradea (although it would have had to be longer), so also did it become evident that evangelical faithfulness to Scripture meant something quite different for Swiss burghers holding at bay the secularized good life compared to Romanian Baptists who gave up chances for higher education and decent jobs when they attended church.

In 1991 it struck us that the ethnic Hungarians in Romania were considerably more isolated than the Romanian Baptists. The Baptists had enjoyed extensive contacts with the West (Wheaton faculty were far from their only visitors, even during the Ceauşescu years). Because the Hungarians' second language was German instead of English, their contacts with the outside world tended to be more formal and ecclesiastical compared to the free-form and entrepreneurial connections that the Baptists had established with the British and Americans. Bob Yarbrough's excellent command of German and my halting efforts left at least one long-lasting impression on this score: it came from an intense conversation with a Hungarian Reformed pastor, conducted in German, discussing the status of his linguistic and religious minority in a country where official communism, deeply-engrained Orthodox culture, and long-standing ethnic tensions made for considerable difficulties. When we asked if there were any blessing from God in these circumstances, the answer was memorable: "The blessing is the difficulties themselves since they are the occasion for God to meet our needs day by day and so to give us occasions for praising his name."

This answer was pious in words entirely conventional in my home setting. In Cluj-Napoca, they sounded anything but conventional.

During the 1991 trip we were also struck with the abundance of new opportunities and new perils that confronted the Romanian Baptists. They now were able to establish specifically Christian institutions—periodicals, primary schools, even their own university—that had simply been impossible only shortly before. They now could send young men for formal seminary training. Some advanced students had already left for graduate study in England, Wales, and the United States. They remained earnest about spiritual matters in ways to shame most Americans. Some of the leaders were developing grand plans to inject spiritual influence into the life of their country. Many also were engaged directly with what they described as the "Orthodox character" of their country. We heard the sentiment consistently expressed that the evangelicals, who had existed in Romania for only a few generations, should be learning at least some things from the Orthodox, whose history stretched back to antiquity (we also learned that other Baptists did not share these opinions but continued to look upon everything Orthodox as either blatantly nonbiblical or hopelessly compromised by cooperation with the Communists). Still, discussions about how to bring the best of Orthodox and evangelical traditions together revealed a rapidly expanding theological maturity.

Yet perils of a new kind also proliferated. Now liberated from Communist constraints, some of these eager evangelicals seemed bent on uncritical adoption of Western ways—busyness as a substitute for reflection, empire building instead of integrity, supremacy instead of servanthood, success defined by numbers instead of faithfulness. This conclusion, it is important to stress, was not so much ours as the message we heard from many with whom we spoke. Everyone blessed God that Ceaușescu was no more, but many seemed as much apprehensive as quickened by the new freedoms they enjoyed.

One reason for apprehension was that the leaders we met were busy to the point of exhaustion. They were flooded with foreign visitors, including us Wheaton professors. They were working nonstop to create, finance, and organize new institutions. They were quarreling among themselves. Quite a few laymen and women were now laboring much longer hours at jobs that were not simply exercises in make-work. A few were taking advantage of the opportunity to earn, for the first time, real money. The removal of the oppressive, anti-Christian dictator, in other words, was an unalloyed blessing, but the new circumstances following that removal not necessarily so.

What I should have been thinking about more than I did at the time was the relationship between authentic Christian faith and the effects of environment on that faith. How were believers moving the culture, avoiding the culture, transcending the culture, reflecting the culture? These questions, I see more clearly now than at that time, concerned not just the "application" of Christian faith but its very essence.

Finally, there was the role of Don Church. Don was the key figure in precipitating these cross-cultural contacts, which were eventually institutionalized with the support of the Wheaton College Alumni Association. Under his gentle prompting these contacts soon spread out beyond Eastern Europe to several other parts of the world. While the college worked slowly through standard official procedures to internationalize the curriculum and educate its constituencies about life beyond American borders, Don cut corners and simply forged ahead to make it happen among some of the faculty.

For the promotion of cross-cultural understanding, this straightforward football and track coach had opened the door to the world. With a can-do attitude and a why-wait mentality, his distinctly American evangelical faith carried him along as he perceived a need and then tried to meet it. With his willingness to let Romanians call the shots for the faculty he sent over, he was modeling the kind of Christian partnership that relativized the influence of Western money and models. Don Church accomplished this great service to Wheaton College, and to Christian believers in other parts of the world, without pausing to spell out theories of culture or theologies of mission. Yet even as Don was pushing me to take part, other voices were showing that, if someone looked for theory or theology, both were ready to hand.

❖ 9 ❖

Moving Out III

In June 1986, Andrew Walls arrived at Wheaton to lecture at a conference organized by Joel Carpenter and Wilbert Shenk of Fuller Theological Seminary. Papers from that conference were later published in a book from Eerdmans, *Earthen Vessels: American Evangelicals and Foreign Missions* (1990), that brought new sophistication—neither hagiographical nor debunking—to the study of mission history. Before that meeting, I may have heard Joel mention Andrew Walls, but I'm quite sure I had read nary a word from him or about him. Walls lectured at Wheaton on the American dimension of the modern missionary movement but only after apologizing for knowing so little American history. The diffidence was as characteristic as the impact of what he said was transformative. From that 1986 conference onward a lodestar had arisen for me.

❖

Andrew Walls was born of Scottish parents in New Milton, England, in 1928.[1] He studied theology and church history at Oxford in

1. Much information and personal insight is found in *Understanding World Christianity: The Vision and Work of Andrew F. Walls*, ed. William R. Burrows, Mark R.

the early 1950s, served a stint as librarian of the evangelical Tyndale House in Cambridge, and was also commissioned as a Methodist "local (or lay) preacher." In 1957 Walls left Britain for Fourah Bay College, Sierra Leone, where he soon made a personal discovery whose effects have reverberated around the globe:

> I arrived in West Africa in my thirtieth year, with an assignment to teach those in training for the ministry in Sierra Leone, and in particular to be responsible for teaching them church history. I had received, as I thought, a pretty good theological education; and my graduate work had been in patristics at Oxford. . . . I shared the conventional wisdom of the 1950s . . . that church history was full of lessons to be imparted to the "younger churches" from the accumulated wisdom of the older ones.
>
> I still remember the force with which one day the realization struck me that I, while happily pontificating on that patchwork quilt of diverse fragments that constitutes second-century Christian literature, was actually living in a second-century church. The life, worship and understanding of a community in its second century of Christian allegiance was going on all around me. Why did I not stop pontificating and observe what was going on?[2]

In Fourah Bay, Walls was discovering that the recent history of Christianity was as dynamic—and was encountering as many new cultural situations—as the ancient history, which by constant repetition had lost its ability to startle.

After further years in Sierra Leone, and then in Nsukka, Nigeria, where he helped establish a new Department of Religion, Walls in 1966 returned to Scotland and a teaching post at the University of Aberdeen. The Aberdeen faculty would soon become the best place anywhere to study what was still at that time the undefined subject of "world Christianity." It came to include, besides Walls, Harold Turner (pioneering student of African Independent Churches), Adrian Hastings (author of several exemplary histories of African Christianity),

Gornik, and Janice A. McLean (Maryknoll, NY: Orbis, 2011), including a valuable bibliography of Walls's writing on pp. 257–77.

2. Andrew F. Walls, introduction to *The Missionary Movement in Christian History: Studies in the Transmission of Faith* (Maryknoll, NY: Orbis, 1996), xiii.

and a young Lamin Sanneh (expounder of paradigm-shifting theories and empirical studies on translation).

Outside the classroom Andrew preached regularly on Methodist circuits and also took a deep interest in Aberdeen society. In 1970 he ran unsuccessfully for Parliament as a Labour candidate; more successful were his efforts on behalf of local arts and artisans. For that service, and about the time of his visit to Wheaton, he was honored with the Order of the British Empire.

In 1982 Walls was the key figure in founding Aberdeen's Centre for the Study of Christianity in the Non-Western World where he directed the doctoral study of several individuals who would themselves become leading promoters of cross-cultural Christian understanding. They included Kwame Bediako, founder of the Akrofi-Christaller Institute for Theology, Mission, and Culture in Akropong, Ghana, and Jonathan Bonk, longtime editor of the *International Bulletin of Missionary Research*, the premier journal for general attention to modern international Christianity. Walls's own efforts at dissemination included his founding of the *Journal of Religion in Africa* and the *Bulletin of the Scottish Institute of Missionary Studies*.

After surviving a second serious heart attack in 1985, and in response to economizing efforts in British higher education, he transferred the Centre to the University of Edinburgh where he continued to expand library and archival collections he had begun at Aberdeen. These collections, which gathered material from the far corners of the globe that would otherwise have perished, remain crucial for ongoing study of Christianity around the world. As does the Centre itself—now under the capable direction of Brian Stanley, whose books on British missions, the 1910 Edinburgh Missionary Conference, and the recent history of English-speaking Protestant evangelicals continue the work that Walls began. In Edinburgh, Andrew's students included another extraordinary crop of scholars, many of whom have gone on to significant labors in world Christian history, including Jehu Hanciles (Emory University), Diane Stinton (Regent College, Vancouver), Timothy Tennant (Asbury Theological Seminary), and Cyril Okorocha (former Anglican primate of Nigeria).

In 1996 Walls "retired" from his Edinburgh post, but only to embark on an ambitious schedule of lecturing, visiting professorships, and miscellaneous encouragement for a far-flung network of students, friends, colleagues, and world Christian neophytes. These labors have taken him to some of the best-known institutions of higher learning in the Western world as well as to entirely unrecognized outposts in the Global South. The two books that have collected his essays and lectures, both published by Orbis, represent only highlights of his scholarship: *The Missionary Movement in Christian History: Studies in the Transmission of Faith* (1996) and *The Cross-Cultural Process in Christian History: Studies in the Transmission and Appropriation of Faith* (2002). With their perceptive analyses of general historical themes and insightful papers on individual missionaries and historians, the books are especially noteworthy for their seminal essays on African Christianity. Few who read these essays or have had the privilege of hearing Andrew Walls lecture in person have come away unchanged.

❖

Others may document their indebtedness to Andrew Walls differently, but for me—as a historian and a Christian—three insights have been crucial. First: the record of Christian communities, as well as the biblical record, reveal that Christianity has always acted in history as both a *particular* and a *universal* faith, and at the same time. In other words, Christianity has always been adapting to specific times, regions, and cultures, but with a recognizable measure of commonality wherever it appears. The elements of that commonality are worship of the God of Israel, "the ultimate significance of Christ," belief in God's activity among his people, recognition of God's people as an entity transcending time and space, common deference to the Scriptures, and ceremonies involving bread, wine, and water.[3]

Walls has explained the combination of particularity and universality through a helpful pair of metaphors. "Church history has always been a battleground for two opposing tendencies; and the reason is

3. Walls, "Culture and Coherence in Christian History," in *Missionary Movement*, 24–25.

that each of the tendencies has its origin in the Gospel itself." The first tendency is the foundational gospel truth that God in Christ "accepts us as we are, on the ground of Christ's work alone." But if we are accepted "as we are," it must include the conditioning we have received "by a particular time and place, by our family and group and society, by 'culture.'" Because of this kind of acceptance, Christian history always records "the desire to 'indigenize,' to live as a Christian and yet as a member of one's own society, to make the Church . . . *A Place to Feel at Home.*"

At the same time, however, another force strains against—even seems to contradict—this indigenizing principle. "Not only does God in Christ take people as they are: He takes them in order to transform them into what He wants them to be." Walls calls this second tendency "the pilgrim principle." It reminds believers constantly that they have "no abiding city," that faithfulness to Christ will lead to tension within the believers' society, since all societies, wherever and whenever in the world, need repentance and redirection every bit as much as individuals. These tensions, however, arise "not from the adoption of a new culture" as such, "but from the transformation of the mind towards that of Christ."[4] To understand that all expressions of Christianity represent both indigenization within local cultures and potential critique of that culture is to grasp something extremely important about the unfolding of the faith in history.

A second insight is Walls's understanding of how the cross-cultural movement of Christianity into new regions has always stimulated Christian theology. This insight has proven especially valuable for showing that the whole history of Christianity, with its limitless array of local situations, can (despite extraordinary diversity) still display unusual coherence. The insight is that the cross-cultural spread of Christianity into new regions has always stimulated fresh Christian theology that often ends up nurturing the whole Christian church. Thus, for efforts to grasp the recent world history of Christianity, we can observe that even with much that is genuinely new, modern

4. Walls, "The Gospel as Prisoner and Liberator of Culture," in *Missionary Movement*, 7–8.

developments outside the Western world also still replicate much that has occurred over the centuries in Western Christian experience.

On the one hand, it is certainly the case that the cross-cultural spread of Christianity prompts new questions, both practical and theoretical. In the sixteenth and early seventeenth centuries, Jesuit missionaries to China, India, and North America had to wrestle with how they should translate biblical names for God (with words already present that represented deities in these cultures, or with neologisms to avoid inappropriate syncretism?). Evangelical missionaries in twentieth-century sub-Saharan Africa had to confront questions from new converts about why the revered patriarchs of the Old Testament had multiple wives, not an issue that most of the missionaries had pondered at any length in Bible school or seminary.

Yet, on the other hand, theological patterns do repeat in history. As an example, the conversion of Europeans to Christianity involved momentous "power encounters," as when Boniface in the early eighth century felled the Oak of Thor—and nothing happened! Similarly, the twentieth-century history of Christianity throughout Asia, Africa, the Pacific Islands, and Latin America has involved countless demonstrations of God's immediate presence overcoming evil spirits and other nonmaterial forces. Contemporary questions in China and much of Africa about how new Christian believers should regard their ancestors create discussions that parallel early Christian debates about how to regard the morally noble heroes of Greek and Roman history.

Regarded more generally, it has always been obvious that as biblical religion moved out of the Semitic culture of ancient Palestine, it had to be adjusted, or translated, in such a way as to communicate effectively in the Greek and Roman cultures that dominated the Mediterranean region in the first Christian century. That effort involved the kind of cultural adaptations with which students of the early Christian creeds are completely familiar. We begin with the biblical message of an active God who reaches out to humanity by calling Israel into covenant and then becoming incarnate in Jesus Christ. But how could that account respond to Greco-Roman questions about what kind of "person" Jesus was, whether his "essence" was divine or human, and what it has meant for humanity to share the same "nature" with the Son of God? The earlier effort at answering such questions resulted in doctrines (as expressed in the Nicene Creed or the Chalcedonian definition of Christ's person) that continue to enrich Christian communities throughout the whole world.

In the same way, we may also expect similar enrichment for all believers everywhere from pastoral and theological responses to the pressing questions that now arise from communities and cultures that are in the same relative position to the Christian message that the Greeks and Romans were when missionaries like the apostle Paul proclaimed the good news to them. There are many such questions. For example, what about the possibility of salvation for family members who lived before the gospel came to a community, when that community understands what it means to be a person only in relation to the ancestors? Or what does Christian faith mean in a globalized economy where unprecedented social dislocation and the awareness of gross inequalities of wealth press in as hard on new Christian communities today as questions about eating food offered to local idols or participating in the "games" at the Colosseum pressed in on new believers in the early centuries? Andrew Walls does not try to answer all such questions, but he has provocatively demonstrated how important they are.

A third insight I have taken from Andrew Walls, and for me the most compelling, is the awareness that "world Christianity" displays the essential character of Christianity itself. In a word, cross-cultural adaptation has been essential wherever Christianity flourishes because *Christianity itself* began and continues through the divine gift of cross-cultural communication: The incarnation, as Walls explains, means that "the Word becomes flesh . . . the Word was made *human*." Christian theology is based on the belief that "Christ was not simply a loanword adopted into the vocabulary of humanity; he was fully translated, taken into the functional system of the language, into the fullest reaches of personality, experience, and social relationship." When humans respond properly to this divine initiative, the result is conversion, "the opening up of the functioning system of personality, intellect, emotions, relationship to the new meaning, to the expression of Christ." Implications for understanding the history of Christianity proceed naturally: "Following on the original act of translation in Jesus of Nazareth are countless re-translations into the thought forms and cultures of the different societies into which Christ is brought as conversion takes place."[5]

Used in this way, and as developed even more extensively in the work of Lamin Sanneh, "translation" can be viewed as a wide-ranging reality that describes the cross-cultural communication of words, concepts, and values.[6] It means that one way of living out, or of speaking, the gospel, with all the cultural particularities that attend the use of specific languages, is carried over into another way of living, another way of speaking, into all the cultural particulars that attend the use of the receptor language. Translation understood in this broad sense has been foundational for the flourishing of Christianity—from the biblical world into Greek and Roman culture (westward) as well as into Syrian and Mesopotamian culture (eastward), then into northern Europe, then the Americas, now into the uttermost parts of the earth. This understanding of God in Christ being translated into our world means that the history of Christianity constantly unfolds new depths and new understanding of the Christian faith itself. To quote Walls once more, "It is a delightful paradox that the more Christ is translated into the various thought forms and life systems which form our various national identities, the richer all of us will be in our common Christian identity. The Word became flesh, and dwelt among us—and we beheld *his* glory, full of grace and truth."[7]

With diffidence and humility Andrew Walls has suggested that all expressions of Christian faith are at the same time both culturally specific and embody the universal in the particular, that cross-cultural communication is the spark that feeds the flame of theology, and that

5. Walls, "The Translation Principle in Christian History," in *Missionary Movement*, 28.

6. Lamin O. Sanneh, *Translating the Message: The Missionary Impact on Culture* (Maryknoll, NY: Orbis, 1989; expanded ed., 2009).

7. Walls, "Culture and Conversion in Christian History," in *Missionary Movement*, 54.

this cross-cultural process is the mirror of the incarnation itself. These insights have constituted a great gift to all who marvel at the recent spread of Christian faith throughout the world.

❖

After Andrew Walls lectured at Wheaton College in June 1986, it took a few years for that address, "The American Dimension of the Missionary Movement," along with related material I was reading from Walls and other historians, to sink in. But when it did sink in, my approach to the history of Christianity in *the United States and Canada* changed forever, and I believe for the better. The same process led to seeing how what I had long been studying as an American historian might actually be relevant to the rest of the world.

❖10❖

Missiology Helping History

Beginning with Andrew Walls, and then broadening out to other helpful authorities like those profiled in chapter 12, I found that thinking about world Christianity brought an unexpected bonus. That bonus was a fresh perspective on historical work in general. Chronology is confused from this point of the memoir forward since for almost thirty years now insights have been tumbling in rapidly—from books, students, conversations, personal experience, and regular reading of the *Economist*, the *New York Review of Books*, and the Bible—while questions about world Christianity percolated in the back of my mind. But one of the first ways I began to see the difference "world Christianity" might make was in thinking about the nature of written history itself.

As a believer aware of contentious modern debates concerning the status of historical knowledge, I had been trying to take the measure of those debates for many years. Yet for focusing those efforts, nothing was as helpful as thinking about the history of Christianity as a worldwide, cross-cultural phenomenon. Thus, when asked in 1995 to address the American Society of Missiologists, I thought I could show how insights from Andrew Walls and his ilk could address dilemmas

of modern historical writing. Abridged and updated, that talk has
now become this chapter.[1]

❖

Missiological perspectives became especially helpful for two matters. First: historical causation could be viewed—at one and the same
time—as a theological exercise and an empirical effort. Second: the
dilemmas of modern historical writing could be at least partially
resolved by following missiological perspectives.

On the first question, missiologists provided a key to the all-impor-
tant connection between history considered as a function of Christian
truth understood only by believers and history considered as a general
social science open to all humanity. Yet to indicate how missiology
could be so important for holding these two together requires a little
background.

Serious academic history writing by Christian believers, which
began in the 1930s and 1940s, has become a veritable deluge during
the last few decades. Pioneers in the mid-twentieth century included
the British Methodist Herbert Butterfield, the Canadian student
of classical culture Norris Cochrane, the Catholic historian of the
Middle Ages Christopher Dawson, the noted historian of the Reformation E. Harris Harbison, and the historian of missions Kenneth
Scott Latourette. More recently the tide has swelled with Lutherans, Anglicans, evangelicals, Catholics, and many more who write
about almost all periods of the church's history and from almost
all perspectives.

Most of these Christian historians have made a strategic adjustment
that opened a door to their participation in the Western university
world. This adjustment was to abandon—at least while working with
standard academic conventions—the tradition of providential historiography. This adjustment required Christian historians to consider

1. Different versions have been published as "The Challenge of Contemporary
Church History, the Dilemmas of Modern History, and Missiology to the Rescue,"
Missiology 24 (January 1996): 47–64; and "The Potential of Missiology for the Cri-
ses of History," in *History and the Christian Historian*, ed. Ronald A. Wells (Grand
Rapids: Eerdmans, 1998), 106–23.

history writing as part of the sphere of creation rather than the sphere of grace, as a manifestation of general rather than special revelation. Put differently, Christian historians have often taken their place in the modern academy by treating history not as theology but as empirical science. This choice meant that they have constructed their historical accounts primarily from facts ascertained through documentary or material evidence and explained in terms of natural human relationships. For these purposes, believing historians have not presumed to show directly how overarching theological realities are played out in details of historical development.

Usually without defining their theoretical commitments explicitly, these historians have hewn to a middle course. Most Christian historians who today find themselves in the academy have gone about their work under the assumption that ordinary historical research cannot reveal God's mind for past events in the way that the inspired writers of Scripture did. They also assume that the primary purpose of historical writing is not apologetics or evangelism. On the other side, however, they have also refused to reduce religious belief and practice to supposedly more basic human conditions. That is, even as academic Christian historians gave up the extremes of providential history, they have also opposed the modern tendency to treat religion as expressing deeper, more fundamental realities.

For such academic Christian historians, students of world Christianity offer a particular kind of assistance. Missiologists now are well positioned to show other Christian historians how to balance the demands of history as theology with the tasks of history as science.

They are in this position because missiologists focus primarily on situations where, in the words of the preface to an outstanding collection of missionary biographies, believers attempt "to effect passage [for others] over the boundary between faith in Jesus Christ and its absence."[2] Such situations almost always entail the widest possible cultural consequences, some recognized at the time, others unanticipated by either missionaries or those to whom the message

2. Gerald H. Anderson, ed., *Mission Legacies: Biographical Studies of Leaders of the Modern Missionary Movement* (Maryknoll, NY: Orbis, 1994), xii.

is brought. These situations, moreover, often witness intense spiritual conflict, both with respect to individuals and the future of societies.

Such missionary situations, in other words, need to be described with simultaneous attention to the meaning of Christianity and to the record of actual human experiences. Missiologists writing about such matters are usually keenly aware of spiritual realities, and so are in a position as Christians to check the tendency in modern historiography to write as if God did not matter. Yet missiologists are also usually alert to the profound cultural dynamics at work in any cross-cultural religious proclamation. As such, they realize that in order to write the history of such encounters it is necessary to pay the most exacting attention to actual human actions, linguistic practices, ideological frameworks, political superstructures, and social consequences. The functional atheism of the academy often makes it difficult for missiologists to keep realities of the faith in focus. The functional gnosticism of sending churches often makes it difficult to keep the realities of lived human experience in view. Yet missiologists, if they can attend to the actual dynamics of what they study, should be able to keep both atheism and gnosticism at bay.

It can be difficult for missiologists, as well as for other Christian historians, to show how the worlds of faith and historical science can be brought together with integrity. Yet because of what they study—situations where unseen spiritual dynamics and visible cultural consequences exist so inextricably entwined—missiologists are in a favored position. Other believers at work on standard historical, or even church historical, topics have made a good beginning at differentiating between history as a function of empirical inquiry and history as a function of theological deductions. We have even begun the task of showing why approaching the past with empirical questions uppermost can be a valid Christian vocation.[3] What we have not done so well is to show how the realms of history-as-science and history-as-theology may coexist or mutually support each other. Perhaps that

3. Such efforts are explored in a chapter entitled "Christology: A Key to Understanding History," in Mark A. Noll, *Jesus Christ and the Life of the Mind* (Grand Rapids: Eerdmans, 2011), 75–98.

inability arises from reactions against the excessive providentialism of earlier Christian history. Yet if balance can be found—between the realms of faith and sight, between the dogmatic overstatements of the past and the confused possibilities of the present—it will probably be missiologists who find it. They will be able to lead the way because of the sensitivities they have developed as historians of faith, historians of culture, and historians of the interactions between faith and culture.

❖

On the second matter, I have also grown impressed with what missiological perspectives might offer historical understanding in general. For a number of reasons—ideological, national, professional, social, and economic—Western thinking about historical knowledge remains in a confused and troubled condition. Worried essays about the epistemological crises of history are not as common as only a few years ago, but uncertainty still hangs in the air as a response to radically unsettling theories—mostly about how language relates to reality—that swept through Western universities from the 1960s. To complicate matters, the newer views have not simply replaced the old. Rather, radical new proposals now contest the terrain with remnants of older views. The result is a field of combat where, to simplify, at least three general positions struggle for ascendancy—the premodern, the modern, and the postmodern—or, more precisely, the ideological, the scientific, and the deconstructive.

The premodern or ideological stance assumes that historical writing exists in order to illustrate the truth of propositions known to be true before study of the past begins. Throughout the past, this approach has always been the most widely practiced kind of history. Herbert Butterfield once memorably called this way of encountering the past, "Whig History," meaning that history is supposed to show how similar all of the past is to the present and how clearly the past reveals the inevitable emergence of those whom we ourselves most favor in the present.[4] Marxists, who explain every historical event as

4. Herbert Butterfield, *The Whig Interpretation of History* (1931; repr., New York: Norton, 1965).

somehow a struggle for control of the means of production, are often criticized for letting ideology triumph over research. But this general approach has prevailed far beyond Marxist circles. The most influential early church historians, Eusebius and Orosius, were also primarily ideologues in this sense since they wrote in order to show how God had ordained the confluence of Jewish-Christian and Roman histories for the universal spread of the church. This premodern conception of history prevailed among Christians in the Middle Ages. It has been a stock-in-trade of competing Christian denominations—Catholics versus Protestants, Protestants versus one another—to the present day. It is probably the most widely practiced form of Christian history, for it specializes in exploiting historical data to show why my theological position or ecclesiastical group is right and my opponents are wrong.

In other venues, premodern history is one of the most potent allies of nationalistic bloodlust. Under the influence of romanticism, ideological history flourished in the nineteenth century as an effort to discover the distinctive *Geister* of the individual European *Völker*, or tribes. This approach has also been important for the self-conception of American historians. Puritans traced the rise of God's kingdom in the howling American wilderness, nineteenth-century historians described the rise of an ideally free and democratic society, the first generation of professional historians in the early twentieth century proclaimed that "Democracy is the only subject for history," and divergent voices in the recent past have read American history as a nurturing cradle for liberating capitalism or materialistic racism. To the extent that these views are dominated by what the historians know to be true before they start ransacking the past for examples, they are ideological.

Another way of referring to this approach is to call it tribal history, which evangelical historian Grant Wacker has described in the following terms: "This is scholarship that is fashioned with private or factional or parochial or ethnic—in a word, nonpublic—criteria of what counts for good evidence, reliable warrants, and sound conclusions. Tribal history rarely suffers from factual inaccuracy in the strict sense of the term. Rather the problem usually proves the opposite: an

inordinate attention to details, but all linked by explanatory frameworks that only insiders find credible."[5]

Although premodern or ideological history has few defenders in
the academy, intellectuals are no less prone to this form of history
than the not so intellectual. The key to a premodern stance is its instinctive, nonreflective partisanship. Premodern history may engender
prodigious research, but it is research with a purpose, and a purpose
firmly fixed before the research even begins.

By contrast, the modern or scientific approach holds that genuine
knowledge of the past must be derived through verificationist procedures modeled directly on a strictly empirical conception of the
physical sciences. This position no longer exercises the dominance it
once enjoyed but nonetheless retains considerable influence among
both academics and the public at large. When a Lincoln biographer
of a previous generation, Albert J. Beveridge, claimed that "facts
when justly arranged interpret themselves" or when his contemporary, Moses Coit Tyler, opined that as a scientific historian he and
his colleagues could "write the whole absolute truth of history," they
illustrated the self-confidence of this approach.[6]

Philosophers and historians of science, not to speak of most practicing historians, have long since abandoned this position, at least in
its extreme forms, but it lingers on, especially among historians who
retain a naïve conception of the scientific method. It also feeds off a
popular perception of history among the public at large. Often due
to pedestrian teaching, some students have been left with the impression that history means a faceless regiment of meaningless potentates
arranged across an iron grid of random dates.

A third position, the postmodern or deconstructive, came from
perceptive thinkers who have made a special point of demonstrating
how all historical writing always has been inherently political. They

5. Grant Wacker, "Understanding the Past, Using the Past: Reflections on Two
Approaches to History," in *Religious Advocacy and American History*, ed. Bruce
Kuklick and D. G. Hart (Grand Rapids: Eerdmans, 1997), 169.

6. Documentation for these and similar statements can be found in Mark A. Noll,
"Scientific History in America: A Centennial Observation from a Christian Point of
View," *Fides et Historia* 14 (1981): 21–37.

have read carefully the works of the first great professional historians in nineteenth-century Europe, where the passage of time reveals how clearly such leaders wrote to heighten the rising sense of nationalism among the European peoples. Just as clear in our own day has been the influence that political considerations (in the broad sense of the term) exert on historical writing. One much-debated example has been efforts in the West to write about the Cold War. Leftist historians followed the evidence and assigned substantial responsibility for the Cold War to the United States; right-wing historians followed the evidence and assigned substantial responsibility to the Soviet Union. Similar have been efforts to write the history of homosexuality. Where gay liberationists find widespread acceptance of such practices in the past, defenders of traditional values find persistent opposition.

Political intent, in these broad terms, also marks writing by church historians. An immense distance, for example, separates the severe tone of Roman Catholic histories of the Reformation written before the Second Vatican Council, which asked Catholics to exercise greater charity in evaluating other groups of Christians, and the much kinder histories of the Reformation written by Catholics after Vatican II. Even historians with their noses deeply buried in the archives can recognize that more is at work when they construct their historical accounts than simply letting the facts fall where they may.

A respected book by three distinguished scholars, Joyce Appleby, Lynn Hunt, and Margaret Jacob, *Telling the Truth about History* (1994), provided a readable summary of these new challenges. According to the authors:

> In the decades since World War II the old intellectual absolutisms have been dethroned: science, scientific history, and history in the service of nationalism. In their place—almost as an interim report—the postwar generation has constructed sociologies of knowledge, records of diverse peoples, and histories based upon group or gender identities. . . . The postwar generation has questioned fixed categories previously endorsed as rational by all thoughtful men, and has denaturalized social behavior once presumed to be encoded in the very structure of humanness. As members of that generation, we routinely, even angrily, ask: Whose

history? Whose science? Whose interests are served by those ideas and those stories? The challenge is out to all claims to universality.[7]

After I had begun to read books by historians studying the world-wide spread of Christian faith, this challenge seemed less daunting than before. For the tribe of Christian believers, missiologists are the ones best positioned to work simultaneously with aspects of the premodern, the modern, and the postmodern.

Missiologists resonate with the premodern in their sympathy with sending churches and receiving cultures, where constructs from the academy—whether modern or postmodern—make almost no sense at all. Missiologists themselves usually believe that something like a direct knowledge of God—whether expressed in terms of the Holy Spirit, the sacraments, or in other ways—is not only possible but is in fact the heart of life itself. Missiologists who share these aspects of the premodern worldview are surely in a position to write about it when they find it in others.

But missiologists are also modern because they see how standards of objectivity have made it possible for Catholic researchers and Protestant researchers to benefit from each other's insights, and together to benefit from the research insights of many who are not Christian in any sense. Missiologists who recognize such gifts as the contributions of modern or scientific historical study are surely in a position to write as moderns themselves.

But missiologists, because they study other cultures and study them with cross-cultural sensitivity, are also primed to benefit from the insights of postmodernity. Their intense focus on the diverse incarnations of the gospel in cultures very different from each other reinforces postmodern awareness of the relativity of knowledge. Missiologists who find valid insights in postmodern history are surely in a position to write with heightened savvy about what they see.

In the end, however, missiologists are not defined primarily as premoderns, moderns, or postmoderns. They continue to be defined

7. Joyce Appleby, Lynn Hunt, and Margaret Jacob, *Telling the Truth about History* (New York: Norton, 1994), 3.

above all else as believing Christians. That ultimate identification preserves them from the bloodlust of ideology, the desiccation of scientific pretense, and the silence of deconstructive solipsism.

It is, I realize, a heroic task that I am assigning to students of cross-cultural Christian history. But they are already leading believing historians geographically—out beyond tight preoccupations with Europe and North America. They have also begun to show how the history of Christianity can encompass the most diverse expressions of particular cultures. As a result, I have great hope that they may also show the way in historical method. That hope rests ultimately in the fact that they study, and study from so many cultural angles, allegiance to the One who as incarnate deity undertook the ultimate act of cross-cultural communication.

❖ 11 ❖

Courses and Classrooms

Fresh reading, expanding curiosity, historiographical specula-
tion, and a few brief experiences outside the United States
were one thing. Taking up the task of actually putting together
a semester-long course was another. For teaching an impossibly huge
subject like "the recent world history of Christianity," I have been
fortunate to make the attempt at Wheaton College, the University of
Notre Dame, and Regent College (Vancouver). Student constituencies
are naturally different in these venues: in my experience, Wheaton
students were more likely to have participated in short-term mission
trips abroad and to have lived as ex-pats overseas before attending
college; Notre Dame students have been more likely to know pastors
in their local parishes who came from abroad; Regent students have
more likely spent considerable time in China, Taiwan, Singapore, and
Hong Kong. Yet at all three institutions, students seemed comfortable
with the limited goals of such a class. We could note the seismic recent changes in the distribution of the world's Christian population;
we could read a few things from Andrew Walls and others who have
devoted their lives to interpreting the spread of the faith around the
world; we could introduce some history for regions and among peoples
whose names I could not pronounce and whose locations I repeatedly

had to check in reference books (later Wikipedia); the students could do a little focused research on a particular place or problem; and we could think together about the mind-expanding questions raised by what our course surveyed. Although everything in such a class must be carried out on a preliminary, even superficial, level, the results (at least for me) could not have been more illuminating, edifying, and enjoyable.

Tenured full professors get a few privileges not offered as often to less-senior members of the profession. One of them is to take on classes for which the instructor can offer no reasonable evidence of actual preparation. In my case, a class in world Christianity was such a privilege.

❖

Thanks to computer software that allows old files to be transferred to new systems, I still can read a memo dated October 24, 1998, that describes a new course I was proposing to the committee at Wheaton assigned responsibility for approving such requests. The title of what was to be offered to upper-division undergraduates and students in Wheaton's master of theology program reads "World Christianity since the Nineteenth Century." At the time, it took a fair amount of persuasion to convince Wheaton's history and theology departments, the college's Educational Policies Committee, and—not least—myself that we should try such a course. In retrospect, the need could not have been more obvious.

Through the 1980s and 1990s I regularly taught a one-semester, four credit-hour survey of the history of Christianity that stretched from the time of the apostles to the present. This course apportioned about three and one-half weeks each to the early church (through the fifth century), the Middle Ages, the Reformation era (to 1648), and then the modern period. Usually I assigned a general text, a collection of primary source documents, and one substantial monograph for each unit (often a biography like Peter Brown on Augustine or Henry Rack on John Wesley). I have a vague memory that the last couple of times I taught the course we might have read an essay or two by Andrew Walls. Students were asked to prepare a research paper on a subject of their own choosing and to write a final exam.

It was a satisfying course, especially once I'd figured out that beginning class with a prayer from the period under discussion for that day and singing a hymn or two from the same era provided a refreshing complement to the instructor's drone. The students' papers offered special rewards since they regularly took up topics, themes, persons, or questions in which I was also deeply interested. Yet however much zest student work added to the class, the expertise I had acquired through graduate school and many years of teaching this material made it clear (at least to my mind) who was the teacher and who were the students.

It was also true that by the time I tried out this new course, I had enjoyed the service of able student assistants. That service contained its own instructive ironies, however, since my very first assistants at Wheaton—Robert Lackie as an undergraduate, Matthew Floding and John Stackhouse as MA students—were so creatively capable that they set an impossibly high standard for all who followed in their train.

The venture into world Christianity radically changed the student-teacher dynamic and required a different kind of student support. Whatever else this challenge entailed, student assistance was imperative. As the history department wrote in the rationale asking for a change, "Our current course fails particularly with respect to the world-wide expansion of Christianity that is every day more widely recognized as a critical aspect of the whole history of Christianity itself." The rationale went on to explain that in the setup then prevailing, "the expansion of Christianity must be treated as a tidbit in at best one-fourth of the course, which is totally inadequate to a genuine survey of the history of Christianity."

Case closed. Approval secured. But now what?

❖

I offered the class for the first time in the spring of 2000. The syllabus got off to a good start by quoting Acts 11:19–20, a passage that Andrew Walls had singled out to show the cross-cultural sensitivity of the very earliest church: "Now those who were scattered because of the persecution that took place over Stephen traveled as far as Phoenicia, Cyprus, and Antioch, and they spoke the word to no one except Jews. But among them were some men of Cyprus and Cyrene who, on coming to Antioch, spoke to the Hellenists also, proclaiming the Lord Jesus." Why, Walls had asked simply, does the passage say "the Lord Jesus" and not "the Lord Jesus Christ"? His answer: to the Greeks of Antioch, "Christ" (that is, Messiah) was a foreign Hebrew term whose meaning could not be taken for granted in that new setting. It was not for them an indigenous term.

The catalogue description intimated that the instructor knew a lot more than was actually the case: "This course surveys the history of world Christianity since the middle of the nineteenth century. It includes some background on the earlier missionary expansion of the church, but its emphasis is on the transition of Christianity from a Western to a world religion in the last two centuries. Most of the course treats the modern history of Christianity outside of Europe and North America. David Barrett's *World Christian Encyclopedia* is the basic reference book for the material to be covered."

Since I needed as much illumination as the students, for this first run of the course I asked them to prepare an essay-review of a relevant book (and so was pointed to several that I later read, or at least looked at, with real profit). Even more help came from additional writing assignments—first a short outline of the history of Christianity in some non-Western part of the world (a couple of students chose Russia) and then a research paper on some aspect of the modern history of Christianity in that country.

Of course I was thinking ahead. In fact, to this day, some of what I parade as "my own" in lectures comes directly from work that students in that class and later renditions have prepared. If I remember where my lecture notes come from, I try to acknowledge these pioneers. That memory challenge is not a problem where students have written especially striking papers or have explored matters about which my ignorance was complete. But I'm also sure that some of what I now consider "mine" has been lifted without attribution from student work.

As a practical matter, the nature of these assignments in 2000 allowed students to take responsibility for a good bit of the lecturing. Our twice-weekly class met on twenty-eight different Tuesdays and

Thursdays throughout that late winter and early spring. After one period for the midterm exam, two classes given over to lectures from visitors, and then five or six periods where students reported to the class on what they had been reading and researching, I had reduced my duties to preparing less than twenty lectures. Whether I could fill even that reduced number was not a facetious question.

Changes even in the short span of years since 2000 indicate how very rapidly "world Christianity" has become, not exactly a coherent field of academic study, but rather an extraordinarily active venue for research, interpretation, controversy, and discussion. On my part, the scheme for that first attempt rapidly gave way to something more traditional. After a year or two of borrowing research results from students, reading faithfully in the *International Bulletin of Missionary Research*, and having time to get through a few books, I found that almost without trying there was now much more in my notebooks, computer files, and scattered papers than a single semester could accommodate. Almost overnight, it seemed, I had moved from worrying about having enough material to carry off a semester course to worrying about not having enough time to even scratch the surface.

The same applied to bibliographical resources to recommend for student reviews and beginning points for their research. The first couple of years, when students asked for help with books, my response often pointed to the library's standard finding aids. Soon, however, I could help out some of the students with books I owned or knew about. Before long, without ever presuming to have any kind of comprehensive grasp of a rapidly expanding literature, I found that I could help more and more students by pointing them to well-researched, responsibly argued studies of Christian developments in almost every corner of the globe.

A simple comparison suggests something about the tremendous recent boom in serious literature devoted to studying Christianity outside the regions that, until the twentieth century, were the faith's heartlands. In 2000, when students asked for bibliographical help, and I was stumped, it turned out that occasionally the problem was not—surprisingly—with me but that serious books simply did not exist. Today, this problem is much less common. In 2000 I'm not sure I could recommend even a score of books I had heard about, much less read, to help the students with their projects. By contrast, for a class at Regent College (Vancouver) in the summer of 2013 entitled "The Recent World History of Christianity, 1900–2013," it was relatively easy to assemble a much fuller course bibliography of more than one hundred thirty titles: forty-two with general or thematic surveys, seven on Asia excluding China and India, nineteen on China, ten on India, twenty-four on Africa, twelve on Latin America, twelve on European and American connections to the world, and ten reference works. By no means had I read all of these works thoroughly, but at least I knew about them, in many cases had been able to rifle through their pages, or had actually read them cover to cover—and that while spending most of the intervening years attending to my day job teaching and writing about the history of Christianity in North America. Even more, although this list of books was far larger than anything I could have provided in 2000, I was keenly aware that even this expanded bibliography barely nibbled at the vast quantity of responsibly published material now available for students, scholars, and the general public.

❖

Various paths can be taken for introducing the extraordinary scope of the worldwide Christian presence. For me, students marked out my path.

But what did they teach me? In this book's last chapter I try to summarize "what I think I have learned" about the worldwide presence of Christian faith by synthesizing insights from student work. But at this point, in order to show how meaningful that instruction was, I can mention a few gifts of insight from students who enrolled in that first course in the spring of 2000 (I may be adding an item or two from ones who took the class in 2001 or 2002).

One carefully researched paper came from a student who had recently completed short-term missionary work in Thailand.[1] It was

---

1. Gwynneth Neagle, "Christianity and Buddhism in the Thai Context" (paper, Wheaton College, 2000).

a part of the world about which I knew almost nothing. The paper reported on the fairly extensive spread of Christian faith among the mountainous tribal peoples, along with the strong resistance to Christianity among the majority ethnic Thais who were almost all Buddhists. Later I read Andrew Walls on the fact that most large-scale accessions to Christianity within the twentieth century have come from practitioners of primal faiths rather than from other world religions.

One of the class members at strongly evangelical Wheaton had recently returned from study in France, an experience she brokered into insights about Catholic history.[2] From mostly French sources, she wrote on the White Fathers, led by Cardinal Charles Lavigerie, who with his colleagues pioneered Catholic missions in Buganda. She was the first person that I can remember to observe that, although Protestant-Catholic tensions were by no means absent during the late nineteenth century in what is now Uganda, those tensions involved fewer and less systematic standoffs than continued in Europe and North America at the time.

Another student wrote a particularly memorable paper on Rwanda.[3] He was himself an active young evangelist who throughout the course had thrilled to accounts of rapidly spreading charismatic and Pentecostal forms of the faith. Yet why, he asked with an earnestness far beyond his years, did the conversion of Rwanda not prevent the Rwandan genocide of 1994? This question has stayed with me as a goad for trying to discern the difference between Christian conversions, on the one hand, and civilization shaped by deeply Christian values, on the other.

Yet another student outlined the history of Christianity in Cameroon, with special attention to the role that English, French, German, and American missionaries played in that story.[4] He also drew attention to native forms of the faith that, while shaped to some degree by the missionaries, developed with clearly indigenous characteristics.

2. Regrettably, I have forgotten this student's name.
3. The student was Trent Sheppard.
4. The student was Jonathan Blumhofer.

With this paper I was given a running start toward Lamin Sanneh's discussion of translation, to which I turned not long thereafter.

In retrospect, I am as impressed with the depth of insight from student work as I am with the breadth that teaching this course opened up. Yet that breadth too was remarkable. It took me only a short while to realize that the students were opening extraordinary vistas for a stay-at-home college professor. In fact, before too long I was almost ready to try knocking off a great Johnny Cash song:

> I was mindin' my own business 'long the standard academic
>   road
> When along came a committee with an issue 'bout my load:
> "If you're game to spice the academic, Mick, try this one on
>   for size,"
> And so I sent along proposals and soon to my surprise,
>
> I was finding that the trick was anything but funny
> As I soon knew that I could sing along with Johnny,
>
> I've been everywhere, man,
> I've been everywhere, man,
> Crossed the desert bare, man,
> I've breathed the mountain air, man,
> Of travel I've had my share, man,
> I've been everywhere.
>
> I've been to
>
> Albania, Armenia, Algeria, Australia,
> Bangladesh, Malawi,
> Turkey, Palestine, Peru,
> Kosovo, Mexico,
> Romania, Australia, Ethiopia, Tanzania,
> Thailand, Mashonaland, Bechuanaland, New Zealand,
> Gimme a hand,
>
> I've been to
>
> Kenya, Russia, Rwanda, Buganda,
> Zimbabwe, Chile, Brazil,
> Korea, China, Costa Rica,

> Guatemala, Venezuela, South Africa,
> Taiwan, Azerbaijan,
> Solomon Islands, Virgin Islands,
> Vietnam, Taiwan, Japan,
> the Yanomami Amazon,
> it's amazin'.
>
> I've been everywhere.

Remarkably, for every country mentioned in this limp pastiche, I still retain a student paper reporting on the development of Christianity in that country—and that is after saving only what I thought were the very best student efforts.

❖12❖

Experts

Trying to teach courses with titles like "The Recent World History of Christianity," even when aided by capable and curious students, soon introduced me to a nearly limitless supply of factual material about the non-Western world. In order to keep that material from becoming simply a parade of unconnected facts, it was obvious that coherence of interpretation was needed to balance the cornucopia of information. Thankfully, it was reassuring that a great deal of coherence was ready to hand from scholars who had been devoting their full-time energies to explain "world Christianity" long before I lifted up my eyes from North America. Andrew Walls, it turned out, enjoyed capable colaborers. The insights they offered have come in many forms and from many directions. An additional blessing (again, the evangelical cliché for which there is no alternative) has been the opportunity to know many of these experts personally. This chapter sketches an outline of indebtedness to some of those who made it possible to offer students responsible generalizations instead of just a bombardment of data.

❖

A first great stimulus was the scholarship of William Reginald (W. R.) Ward who spent most of his preretirement academic life at the

University of Durham. Ward was a distinguished historian of taxation in eighteenth-century England, the University of Oxford, and English Methodism before he published several books that decisively reoriented study of the evangelical awakenings of the seventeenth and eighteenth centuries.[1] Ward studied those awakenings as no one had done before. He insisted that they be viewed as beginning in Central Europe, maybe even with a children's prayer revival in far-distant Silesia, and then spreading gradually throughout continental Europe and Britain before leaping the Atlantic to the American colonies. With considerable panache, Ward argued that anyone wanting to take the measure of John and Charles Wesley, George Whitefield, Jonathan Edwards, and other well-known revivalists in the English-speaking world simply had to begin with Jakob Böhme, Gottfried Arnold, Pierre Poiret, Gerhard Teerstegen, and other Europeans about whom most scholars in Britain and America knew little. In works of great erudition—and a dauntingly allusive prose style—Ward made good on his claim that Protestant renewal movements from the mid-1600s to the late 1700s were distinguished by their resistance to political, as well as religious, authorities. He was just as convincing in his claim that these movements characteristically advocated experiential personal religion manifest in small-group conventicles of like-minded awakened believers.

For better understanding of world Christianity, Ward provided a welcome stimulation to look farther afield. Even for a subject like the history of modern evangelicalism, which I assumed I knew well, Ward showed how important it was to peer across borders, to read more than just English, to take supposedly marginal groups as seriously as those who saw themselves at the center, and to see that vital Christian movements could never be contained within national borders. Ward's lessons, as an extension of his own research conclusions, were made for traveling—geographically, to be sure, but also conceptually.

1. W. R. Ward, *The Protestant Evangelical Awakening* (New York: Cambridge University Press, 1992); *Faith and Faction* (London: Epworth, 1993); *Kirchengeschichte Großbritanniens vom 17. bis zum 20. Jahrhundert*, trans. Sabine Westermann (Leipzig: Evangelische Verlagsanstalt, 2000); *Early Evangelicalism: A Global Intellectual History* (New York: Cambridge University Press, 2006).

❖

Dana Robert of Boston University expanded on the positive instruction I was receiving from W. R. Ward. About the time of my talk to the
missiologists in the mid-1990s, I was privileged to read a partial draft
of her manuscript on the place of women in the historical development
of missionary theory.[2] The missiological perspective brought to bear
in that work turned on a light that soon illuminated my own work;
later, the bridge she constructed from research in Western sources to
perceptive conclusions about world Christianity helped me make a
similar transition in my own thinking.

Shortly before reading Robert's manuscript on women and mission
theory, I had published a general history of North American Christianity in which I tried to let Christian rather than national norms shape
the narrative. What her manuscript seemed to accomplish so effortlessly
was what I had found so difficult—namely, to write a comprehensive
narrative, fully comparative, and from a broadly Christian rather than
narrowly national or ideological perspective. Her missiological angle of
vision pointed the way, not just to new material, however interesting in
itself, but to a new perspective on the historian's task. That perspective
was global. It also recognized the reality of authorial bias rooted in
the academic culture of modern America but counteracted that bias
by respectful treatment of the cultures that received the missionaries.
With a focus on women, Robert also showed how Christian history
could be written that did not equate the formal actions of denominations and the most visible pronouncements of spokesmen with the
sum of Christian development. Her work provided, in sum, a vision of
history written self-consciously as Christian but also self-consciously
as cultural. Such a history would not depend exclusively on national
or other factors extrinsic to basic Christian concerns. And it would
feature the ordinary lives of ordinary believers yet without neglecting
the formal actions of institutions and nations.

2. Published as Dana Robert, *American Women in Mission: A Social History of
Their Thought and Practice* (Macon, GA: Mercer University Press, 1996). This book
was later supplemented by a fine collection of essays; Robert, ed., *Gospel Bearers,
Gender Barriers: Missionary Women in the 20th Century* (Maryknoll, NY: Orbis, 2002).

Soon thereafter, Robert published the best short summary I know of concerning the dramatic reconfiguration of Christianity over the course of the twentieth century. In this essay for the *International Bulletin of Missionary Research*, entitled "Shifting Southward: Global Christianity Since 1945," she explained why the "forms and structures of late 20th century Christianity could not be contained within either the institutional or the theological framework of Western Christianity." She also offered a telling summary for what her own work and the labors of an increasing number of other scholars made startlingly clear: "The typical late 20th century Christian was no longer a European man, but a Latin American or African woman." Her succinct analysis acknowledged that in Western eyes the world picture during the 1960s and 1970s appeared depressingly confused: some voices in non-Western churches were calling for a missionary moratorium, the World Council of Churches rushed headlong to embrace social advocacy at the apparent neglect of evangelistic proclamation, and the Catholic Church was tied in knots over reactions to the pope's declaration on birth control, *Humanae Vitae*. Yet she pointed out that beyond Western preoccupation with these turmoils, Christianity was expanding at breakneck speed in many non-Western regions of the world. If that explosion of converts and new Christian communities was diverse, often chaotic, multiform, and sometimes anarchic, it nonetheless created a new reality where hope and possibility were just as evident as confusion and retrenchment.[3]

Some years later Robert published a superb short text entitled *Christian Mission: How Christianity Became a World Religion* (Wiley-Blackwell, 2009), which I now regularly assign to classes. Its deft narrative describes the major periods in Christian history as a reflection of missionary endeavor. Its illustrative episodes also show how events of seemingly little weight, in the far reaches of nowhere, have grown in significance as Christianity has spread around the world. The most riveting of such examples concerns Bernard Mizeki—born

3. Dana Robert, "Shifting Southward: Global Christianity Since 1945," *International Bulletin of Missionary Research* 24, no. 2 (April 2000): 50–58 (quotations on pp. 54, 50).

in Mozambique, converted as a youth in Cape Town, South Africa, and then for only a few years an Anglican missionary in Mashonaland (now Zimbabwe). Mizeki was murdered in the early hours of June 18, 1896, by Shona tribesmen caught up in a complex conflict involving British colonists and native antagonists. It was an almost unknown event when it occurred in a part of the world all but unrecognized in Western eyes. Today, tens of thousands Zimbabwean Anglicans gather each year for a pilgrim Communion service on or near June 18 to honor Mizeki's memory. As now members of the Majority Christian world, the pilgrims are celebrating God's work through a pioneer.

At Boston University, Dana Robert has trained a host of doctoral students from around the world who have themselves gone on to explore the meaning of Christian faith in many parts of Africa, Asia, and the Americas. Her instruction has been especially potent for demonstrating how centrally the history of missionary effort defines the history of Christianity, period.

I first encountered the work of Lamin Sanneh when trying to explain a startling feature in the American history of the Bible. For an assignment to write on the presence of Scripture in the United States beyond the main Protestant denominations for the period 1860 to 1925, I discovered an incredible story. Within less than three-fourths of a century, there were published in the United States 136 different editions of English-language Bibles other than the King James Version, the Revised Version, or the American Standard Version. Even more remarkable, during the same period, within the United States, there appeared at least 279 editions of the Bible not in English, including 100 different editions in German, 35 in Spanish, ten each in Danish and Dakota, and four each in Finnish, Gilbertese, Polish, and Zulu.[4]

For making sense out of this profusion of Bible translation and publication, I found that the best resource came from missiological

---

4. Mark A. Noll, "The Bible, American Minority Faiths, and the American Protestant Mainstream," in *Minority Faiths and the American Protestant Mainstream*, ed. Jonathan Sarna (Champaign: University of Illinois Press, 1997), 191–231.

circles. Alongside insights from Andrew Walls, Lamin Sanneh provided a persuasive account of how throughout the history of Christianity the translation of Scripture into local, vernacular tongues had
exerted unexpectedly wide influence for culture formation, as well
as for spreading the faith. Here was a historiography that focused
not on what the missionaries did when they translated, as had the
missionary accounts I knew from decades before, but rather on what
happened among the people who received the Bible in their own language. The acquisition of vernacular Scriptures often accompanied,
as Sanneh has put it, "cultural understanding, vernacular pride, social
awakening, religious renewal, [and] cross-cultural dialogue."[5] For me
the illumination was transformative. Sanneh, with Walls and a few
others, was showing that study of the Bible and minority faiths *in the
United States* would be more productive if I approached the issue as a
missiological problem—that is, if I concentrated on the circumstances
that prompted indigenous editions of the Bible, on the reasons why a
minority group might choose to appropriate the mainstream Bible for
its own purposes, and on the cultural consequences when a Christian
group acquired the Bible in its own language.

In other words, I was finding out that the theory and history that
Sanneh spelled out in his paradigm-changing book from 1989, *Translating the Message: The Missionary Impact on Culture*, could en-
lighten the history of Christianity wherever that history took place.
In that wide-ranging study, Sanneh's argument explained the twofold
dignity that translation conveyed: "First is the inclusive principle
whereby no culture is excluded from the Christian dispensation or
even judged solely or ultimately by Western cultural criteria. Second
is the ethical principle of change as check to self-absorption." In
other words, the history of Bible translation underscores the twofold
character of Christianity itself as fully life-embracing *and* everywhere
a challenge to every aspect of life. As Sanneh himself put it, "Both
of these ideas [inclusive principle, ethical principle] are rooted in
what missionaries understood by God's universal truth as this was

5. Lamin O. Sanneh, *Translating the Message: The Missionary Impact on Culture*
(Maryknoll, NY: Orbis, 1989), 2.

revealed by Jesus Christ, with the need and duty to work out this fact in the vernacular medium rather than in the uniform framework of cultural homogeneity."[6] In addition, missionary translations often worked at cross-purposes with Western imperial intentions, even if the missionary translators saw that result only dimly. Since these translations often undergirded the "emergence of indigenous resistance to colonialism," they profoundly influenced political and social history as well as theological development.[7]

Lamin Sanneh grew up as a Muslim in Gambia, where he was converted to Christianity. Then he received academic training on four continents, became an advisor to the Vatican, and after service in Aberdeen came to Yale University, where he has enjoyed a long career teaching Islamic and African studies as well as world Christianity. His important books, including an autobiography called *Summoned from the Margin: Homecoming of an African* (Eerdmans, 2012), have underscored the importance for all Christian communities of the worldwide character of the faith. That understanding begins, in Sanneh's view, with the New Testament interpreted as a missionary document oriented toward a cross-cultural, pluralistic vision of the kingdom of God. In his words, the teaching of Jesus and his apostles showed that "territoriality [had] ceased to be a requirement of faith."[8]

Sanneh's approach to missionary practice has provided special assistance when I have tried to deal fairly with the responsibility that missionaries bore for heavy-handed, often destructive, Western imperialism. Sanneh does not dispute that "missions were organized, funded, and directed from the West, a fact that made it easy to construe them as colonialism at prayer," but he insists on a "revisionist history" that understands events as always much more than Christianity in service to European empire. In a particularly effective comparison, Sanneh has contrasted the empire building of Cecil Rhodes with the Africa affirmations of David Livingstone. Whereas Rhodes subjugated African workers to imperial ends, Livingstone took the workers' side,

6. Ibid., 208.
7. Ibid., 123.
8. Lamin Sanneh, *Disciples of All Nations: Pillars of World Christianity* (New York: Oxford University Press, 2008), 7.

despite unceasing European criticism of his efforts. After a span of years, the legacy of Livingstone and the missionaries who shared his commitment produced Kenneth Kaunda, Joshua Nkomo, Kamuzu Banda, and the other heralds of African self-determination. They were the ones who eventually transformed Southern and Northern Rhodesia and the other European protectorates established by Rhodes and his ilk: "Rhodes left a legacy of black subjugation under white dominion; Livingstone of irrepressible African aspirations."[9]

Far from an anodyne subject for hazy myth-making, missionary history from scholars like Sanneh turned out to demand attention for its world-historical significance.

❖

A different kind of assistance came to the aid of students and myself from Philip Jenkins, long a professor at Pennsylvania State University who has recently moved to Baylor University. His 2002 Oxford University Press book, *The Next Christendom: The Coming of Global Christianity*, represented a sharp wake-up call for general audiences. The great merit of Jenkins's short, clearly written, yet fact-stuffed book was to synthesize the burgeoning literature on non-Western, or Southern Hemisphere, Christianity and to make bold projections for the twenty-first century. He used what missiologists had been saying in their own circles for some time in order to force the public to sit up and take notice. Jenkins's burden was to reorient the history of Christianity in light of contemporary realities like the following:

- In 1999, there were 18 million Roman Catholic baptisms as recorded by official records of that church—of those baptisms, 8 million took place in Central and South America, 3 million were in Africa, and 37 percent of the African baptisms were of adults.
- For most major Protestant traditions, the largest individual denominations today are located outside of the United States or Europe.
- As of 2000, only three of the world's ten most populous nations (the United States, Russia, Japan) were located in "the West." Using conservative demographic projections that include

9. Ibid., 144.

AIDS-related mortality, it is all but certain that by 2050, twelve of the world's thirteen most populous nations will be in Asia, Africa, and Latin America (the United States as the only exception).

By highlighting such indisputable evidence, Jenkins produced a popular, blunt, and straightforward statement: The center of gravity in world Christianity has moved south. It will almost certainly continue to do so at an accelerated pace. While European Christianity is retreating and North American Christianity survives often as only cultural identification, Christianity in ever-expanding sections of Africa, Latin America, and Asia is dynamic, life-transforming, and revolutionary—if often also wild, ill-informed, and undisciplined. Muslim-Christian conflicts will almost certainly grow in quantity and intensity throughout the twenty-first century as centers of rapid Christian and Muslim expansion encroach on each other in many parts of the two-thirds world.

Jenkins also included a helpful corrective to American and European parochialism about what counts as "news" about the world. In his biting phrases, "When a single racial or religiously-motivated murder takes place in Europe or North America, the event occasions widespread soul-searching, but when thousands are massacred on the grounds of their faith in Nigeria, Indonesia, or the Sudan, the story rarely registers. Some lives are worth more than others."[10]

Just as helpful as the information in Jenkins's book is his insistence that Christian expansion (and also, by implication, Muslim expansion) deserves to be viewed the way the new Christians (or Muslims) describe it. He is, of course, aware that the need for social cohesion among displaced peoples can explain the attraction of Christian community, that massive relocation to cities can explain the attraction of inner self-discipline provided by the Pentecostal experience of God, or that the promise of divine healing for so many individuals without modern health care can explain the attraction of some Christian movements. Jenkins, however, tries very hard to break through the Western insouciance that presumes

10. Philip Jenkins, *The Next Christendom: The Coming of Global Christianity* (New York: Oxford University Press, 2002), 163.

to tell non-Westerners what they are really up to. Whatever political, social, or cultural factors may be appropriate in explaining Christian expansion in the non-Western world, Jenkins holds that "one all-too-obvious explanation is that individuals came to believe the message offered, and found this the best means of explaining the world around them." Likewise, he insists that "people join or convert because they acquire beliefs about the supernatural realm and its relationship to the visible world." In fact, Jenkins insists that amid the great diversity of Christian churches in the Southern world, a common feature is "the critical idea that God intervenes directly in everyday life."[11]

❖

In looking for help to interpret the vast changes in recent Christian history, I soon discovered many younger scholars as well. Representative of a rising tide of insight is Jehu Hanciles, a native of Sierra Leone and one of Andrew Walls's students at Edinburgh who taught at Fuller Theological Seminary for many years before moving to Emory University. These younger scholars are contributing in growing numbers to the burgeoning quantity of carefully researched monographs on historical figures who received little attention during their own lives but who—because of the emergence of their regions as significant areas of Christian expansion—now loom very large. Hanciles added to that stock with impressive work on the missionary strategy of Henry Venn, who, as leader of the Anglican Church Missionary Society in the nineteenth century, defined the central purpose of a missionary as "euthanasia" (or self-elimination). Hanciles has also written perceptively about Samuel Ajayi Crowther, the Nigerian-born translator, preacher, church-planter, and evangelist who, with Venn's support, became the first Anglican bishop in Africa.[12]

Hanciles has gone further, however, by also providing a synthetic study on one of the most powerful engines of Christian development

11. Ibid., 44, 77 (last two quotations).
12. Jehu Hanciles, *Euthanasia of a Mission: African Church Autonomy in a Colonial Context* (Westport, CT: Praeger, 2002); *In the Shadow of the Elephant: Bishop Crowther and the African Missionary Movement* (Oxford: Church Missionary Society, 2008).

in the postwar era. This study, *Beyond Christendom: Globalization, African Migration and the Transformation of the West* (Orbis, 2008), shows how understanding the movement of peoples is crucial for grasping the history of Christianity in Africa—but not only Africa. Increasingly in the modern globalized world, migration defines the history of Christianity everywhere. Mission service now no longer means "The West to the Rest" but "From Everywhere to Everywhere." Hanciles's focus on the general effects of people movements upsets settled opinions about both traditional Western Christianity and Christianity in new places around the world. In other words, he illustrates that careful attention to the actual circumstances of the emerging Christian world adds significantly to what can be known about both Christianity and the modern world.

❖

As it turned out, my search for authoritative interpreters of the recent history of Christianity turned up almost as many thought-provoking voices as I found in looking simply for information. In chapters that follow I detail more of these debts, but here it is important to mention two other authors who, when I was looking for help, provided it. With writing as rich in cultural and theological insight as in historical range, Samuel Hugh Moffett provided a magisterial survey of the long history of Christianity in Asia as well as timely words of personal encouragement.[13] Then David Livingstone helped me see how research and ethnographic reports by missionaries left a permanent imprint on the history of science.[14] And still others, some of whom are mentioned in chapter 17, did more of the same. Together these authorities have presented the Christian past in fresh—nearly revolutionary—ways for those of us with eyes eager to see.

13. Samuel H. Moffett, *A History of Christianity in Asia*, vol. 1, *Beginnings to 1500*; vol. 2, *1500 to 1900* (Maryknoll, NY: Orbis, 1998, 2005 [first vol., orig. 1992]).

14. David N. Livingstone, "Text, Talk and Testimony: Geographical Reflections on Scientific Habits. An Afterword," *British Journal for the History of Science* 38 (2005): 93–100; and more generally, *Putting Science in Its Place: Geographies of Scientific Knowledge* (Chicago: University of Chicago Press, 2003).

❖13❖

By the Numbers

The second edition of David Barrett's *World Christian Encyclopedia* was published in late 2000, shortly after I taught a "world Christianity" survey for the first time. In preparing for that class, I had often turned to the first edition from 1982, especially for its country-by-country surveys and its unusually full chronology of important events in the history of Christianity—from the first disciples to the present and (with conjectures) well into the future. Early in his career, after working as an aeronautics engineer, the British-born Barrett served as an Anglican missionary in Africa where he was one of the first Westerners to write empathetically about the surging number of independent churches that skyrocketed after World War II. Then working from Africa and the United States, Barrett enlisted a worldwide force of correspondents who provided his raw material for the 1982 *Encyclopedia*. As much as that edition provided, a great deal more came in the nearly two thousand over-sized pages of the new edition, this time with the assistance of Todd Johnson and George Kurian. The 1982 edition, published before the breakup of the former Soviet Union and other political fragmentations, contained surveys of 223 countries; the new edition had such information, often expanded, on 238 countries. Even with an asking price of $295, this second edition was a steal.

Before long, however, other careful number crunchers were adding their contributions to the effort at charting a comprehensive world picture. These included an annual statistical survey in the January issue of the *International Bulletin of Missionary Research*, overseen by Johnson with Barrett until the latter's death in 2011 and then with other assistants thereafter; successive editions of *Operation World*, a prayer guide edited most recently by Jason Mandryk with carefully digested information on all the world's countries and, for large countries like China and India, on individual provinces;[1] and then in 2009 a major atlas edited by Johnson and Kenneth Ross.[2]

These sources provide the wherewithal for outlining the dramatic changes that have recently occurred in the Christian world. I have probably overused bullet points (like the following) when starting off a course on recent Christian history or beginning a talk to church audiences. But for anyone who is not numbed by such information, the tectonic shifts these numbers reveal are simply breathtaking.

- Last Sunday, it is probable that more Chinese believers were in church than in all of so-called "Christian Europe"; as recently as 1970 there had been no legally open churches in China.

- Last Sunday, more Anglicans attended church in *each* of Kenya, South Africa, Tanzania, and Uganda than did Anglicans in Britain and Episcopalians in the United States combined (the number of Anglicans at church in Nigeria was several times the number in these other African countries).

- Last Sunday more members of the Pentecostal Assembles of God in Brazil were in church than the combined total of the two largest Pentecostal denominations in the United States, the Assemblies of God and the Church of God in Christ.

- Last Sunday more people attended the Yoido Full Gospel Church in Seoul (founded by pastor David Young-gi Choi and

---

1. Jason Mandryk, ed., *Operation World*, 7th ed. (Downers Grove, IL: InterVarsity, 2010).

2. Todd M. Johnson and Kenneth R. Ross, *Atlas of Global Christianity* (Edinburgh: Edinburgh University Press, 2009).

his mother-in-law Choi Ja-shil) than attended *all* of the churches in significant North American denominations, such as the Christian Reformed Church, the Evangelical Free Church, or the Presbyterian Church in America.

- Last Sunday the churches with the largest attendance in England and France had mostly black congregations. And the largest congregation in all of Europe was the Embassy of the Blessed Kingdom of God for All Nations in Kiev, Ukraine, pastored by the Nigerian-born Sunday Adelaja.

- Among Roman Catholics, the new globalization has been just as obvious. Today the country with the largest contingent of Jesuits is India. More Catholics are active as churchgoers in the Philippines than in any European country. And from early 2013, the new head of the church is a pope from Argentina who, while traditional in his theology, displays passionate commitment to the poor and marginalized—and who, as it happens, also enjoys a record of good relations with evangelical Protestants.

- Today there are perhaps two thousand Christian missionaries working cross-culturally in Britain (and several times that many in the United States)—most with immigrant communities but some to the population in general. There are about twenty thousand Korean missionaries active outside of their country, and perhaps ten thousand from Nigeria. (The comparable US figure is around one hundred thousand, but with many of those short-term missionaries.) Additionally, if a "missionary" is defined as a believer working cross-culturally and cross-linguistically, then there may be as many Chinese and Indian missionaries at work outside of their native regions—yet still in China or India—as missionaries from the United States working overseas.

Obsessive readers who might want to know what I considered the strengths and weaknesses of the 2000 *World Christian Encyclopedia* could read the review I wrote at the time.[3] More important by far, however, is the cumulative impression that David Barrett, Todd Johnson, Jason Mandryk, and other careful enumerators have provided concerning the development of world Christianity over

---

3. The citation is in this book's appendix.

the last century or so. The numbers by themselves can be opaque, intimidating, or off-putting. But when combined with focused local histories, reports of specific Christian movements, and biographical or autobiographical accounts, the numbers create a sounding-board effect. In my classes, I'm not sure I've always stressed enough why looking at such numbers can be helpful. The reason is that they announce changes of great significance, even if it is necessary to find local, particular, and personal witnesses to flesh out the meaning of those changes. Yet especially for someone who grew up mesmerized by batting averages and the electoral margins of state and national elections, the enumerators have assembled more than enough to make my head spin in wonder.

When looking at such numbers it is always important to remember limitations. The most important has been well stated by Leigh Eric Schmidt, who once wrote, "Most of the things that count most about Christianity cannot be counted."[4] Yet it is also important to remember that large, comprehensive enumerations always involve a measure of imprecision. Furthermore, definitions must always be probed carefully to ascertain what researchers mean by a "Christian," a "practicing Christian," a "church member," or, as one of Barrett's categories is called, a "Great Commission Christian." Nonetheless, once all proper qualifications are in place, the aggregate gross statistics still reveal a great deal indeed.

The 2000 *World Christian Encyclopedia* is filled with revealing information. The next several paragraphs provide only a hint of the riches that fill its pages and that also appear in the pages of *Operation World* and the *Atlas of Global Christianity*. But even for the *Encyclopedia*, it is important to remember that its figures reflect calculations for the mid-1990s and that things have careened on at a great pace since that time as well. I include these numbers here because they were

4. Leigh E. Schmidt, "Mixed Blessings: Christianization and Secularization," *Reviews in American History* 26 (1998): 640.

what drove home for me the magnitude of the changes I was trying to describe to my students.

For worldwide Anglicanism, as an example, the *Encyclopedia* reports on the huge numbers in many African countries (Nigeria 17.5 million, Uganda 7.4 million, Kenya 2.7 million, Tanzania 2.3 million), but it also reports on the even larger number of Roman Catholic adherents in these very same countries (except Nigeria, where the Anglicans outnumber the Catholics). The *Encyclopedia* offers a detailed snapshot of the 39 separate Presbyterian denominations in South Korea, the Methodist Church in Fiji that enrolls more than half of the island's population, and the Zion Christian Church of South Africa with its more than 7 million adherents. It profiles Brazil with its sprawling Catholic Church connected to more than 144 million citizens as well as its seven non-Catholic denominations with at least 2 million members each (including the Assembleias de Deus, listed at 22 million).

For those interested in the geographical spread of denominations, the *Encyclopedia* provides a listing of the countries where the various Christian traditions (and Christian-related traditions, such as Jehovah's Witnesses and Mormons) have established a presence. Out of 238 countries, the Roman Catholic Church is found in 235, Jehovah's Witnesses in 212, Seventh-day Adventists in 199, Pentecostals of Baptist or Keswick origin in 178, Baptists in 163, Anglicans in 162, Presbyterian or Reformed in 141, Lutherans in 122, Pentecostals of Holiness origin in 118, Methodists in 108, and Mormons in 102.

A measure of comparative zeal where the *Encyclopedia* shows old-world Christianity to slightly better advantage is the ratio of Christian workers stationed abroad per each million of affiliated Christians. Even if countries with small numbers of Christian adherents can easily rise to the top in such comparisons, it is still instructive to find several traditionally Catholic European countries ranking high alongside countries of recent Christianization. The nine countries the *Encyclopedia* ranks at the top with this measurement are Ireland (2,772 foreign workers per million affiliated Christians), Malta (2,693), Samoa (1,774), St. Pierre and Miquelon (1,565), Palestine

(1,328), Faeroe Islands (1,263), Singapore (1,241), Belgium (1,197), and American Samoa (1,086). Then comes the Netherlands in tenth place (992), Spain in thirteenth (823), New Zealand in fourteenth (820), and Canada in fifteenth (815). Other historic mission-sending countries trail behind, including the United States (619), Switzerland (528), and Norway (428).

In the *Encyclopedia*'s second volume the editors show the number and types of Christians found among the world's ethnic groups, languages, cities, or provinces/states. Intriguing information surfaces in all of these sections, especially from the city survey which records 114 Chinese and 61 Indian cities with at least 10 percent Christian population (remember that these results are from the mid-1990s). The same section records a higher total of Christian adherence for the city Aizawl at 90 percent (Mizoram, India) and the city Kohima at 85 percent (Nagaland, India) than for any city in the United States or the United Kingdom.

For a bird's-eye summary that tries to show the changes for the whole world since 1900, this chapter closes with tables like those I've regularly provided to classes. The first is from the 2000 *Encyclopedia*. It shows that from 1900 to 2000 the number of individuals affiliated with Christian churches in Europe, Latin America, North America, and Oceana rose at roughly the same rate as the general population. By contrast, the number of affiliated Christians in Africa rose about five times faster than the general population, while the number in Asia rose four times as fast.

World Christian Encyclopedia (2000): Affiliated Christians (millions)

	Affiliated Christians			Total Population	
	1900	2000	Multiple	2000	Multiple from 1900
Africa	8.8	335.1	38	784.5	7
Asia	20.8	307.3	15	3,697.0	4
Europe	368.2	536.8	1.5	728.9	1.8
Latin Am.	60.0	440.0	7	519.1	8

	Affiliated Christians			Total Population	
	1900	2000	Multiple	2000	Multiple from 1900
N. Amer.	59.6	203.7	3.5	309.6	4
Oceana	4.3	21.4	5	30.4	5

The second table, also from the *Encyclopedia*, enumerates categories that are defined like this:

Evangelicals (Ev): "A subdivision mainly of Protestants consisting of all affiliated church members calling themselves Evangelicals, or all persons belonging to Evangelical congregations, churches or denominations; characterized by commitment to personal religion."

Charismatics (Pent-Char): "Baptized members affiliated to nonpentecostal denominations who have entered into the experience of being filled with the Holy Spirit; [and] the Second Wave of the Pentecostal-Charismatic-Neocharismatic Renewal."

Great Commission Christians (GCC): "Believers in Jesus Christ who are aware of the implications of Christ's Great Commission, who have accepted its personal challenge in their lives and ministries, are attempting to obey his commands and mandates, and who are seeking to influence the body of Christ to implement it."

For each of these categories, the same phenomenal expansion appears for Africa and Asia.

Evangelical/Pentecostal-Charismatic/Great Commission Christians (millions)

	1900			2000		
	Ev	Pent-Char	GCC	Ev	Pent-Char	GCC
Africa	1.6	.9	3.1	69.6	126.0	90.8
Asia	1.3	0.0	10.5	31.5	134.9	191.9
Europe	32.4	0.0	49.8	21.5	37.6	192.5
L. Am.	.8	0.0	2.4	40.3	141.4	52.3
N. Am.	33.5	0.0	11.6	43.2	79.6	105.3
Oceana	2.2	0.0	.5	4.4	4.3	9.1

The third and fourth tables come from the January 2013 *IBMR*.[5] They underscore how rapidly the Christian population has continued to expand in Africa (170 million additional adherents since the mid-1990s) and in Asia (up 60 million). It also shows that the Catholic Church remains home to about half of the world's identifiable Christians. The fourth table shows why it is now customary to speak of "Global South" Christianity. The proportion of affiliated Christians in Africa, Asia, and Latin America as of 2013 (64 percent of all Christians worldwide) is not yet the proportion found in Europe and North America in 1900 (82 percent), but the time when the former proportion will match—and perhaps exceed—the latter proportion is not far away.

The World-Christian Picture, 2013 (all figures in millions)

	1900	2013	Projected 2025
World population	1,620	7,130	8,002
Muslim population	200	1,635	1,972
Nonreligious	3	684	701
Hindu population	203	982	1,104
Total Christian "count"	558	2,354	2,707
Affiliated church members	522	2,245	
Church attenders	469	1,555	
"Evangelicals"	72	306	
Pentecostals/charismatics	1	628	
"Great Commission Christians"	78	702	
Roman Catholics	267	1,202	
Protestants/Anglicans	134	531	
Orthodox	116	280	
Independent/Marginal	9	417	

5. From Todd M. Johnson and Peter F. Crossing, "Status of Global Mission, 2013, in Context of AD 1800–2025," *International Bulletin of Missionary Research* 37 (January 2013): 32–33.

Affiliated Church Members by Region
(3rd column, % of total Christian population)

	1900	2013	(% 1900–2013)
Africa	8.7	509.6	1.7 – 22.7
Asia	20.8	365.1	4.0 – 16.3
Latin America	60.0	555.6	11.6 – 24.7
Oceana	4.3	24.8	0.8 – 1.1
Europe (including Russia)	365.3	562.3	70.4 – 25.0
North America	59.6	227.6	11.5 – 10.1

Numbers as in these tables are like a megaphone. They cannot explain the momentous shifts in world Christian adherence that have taken place over the last century, but they show beyond a shadow of a doubt that these shifts have occurred.

❖ 14 ❖

Looking South: A Guide

Among statistics spotlighting the dramatic recent changes in world Christianity, one number stands out for many Protestants, especially evangelical Protestants of my background. It is the large figure for Latin America: 60 million identified Christians in 1900, grown to over 550 million in 2013—from less than 12 percent of all Christians in the world to nearly one-fourth. The difficulty posed for evangelicals who share my upbringing is a question about whether these numbers represent genuine believers in any qualitative sense.

In Cedar Rapids we regularly hosted missionaries from Argentina, Ecuador, and elsewhere in Latin America who described great difficulties as they encountered the deeply engrained Catholic cultures of the region. Frequently we heard stories of active persecution, often of poverty-stricken Indian congregations who had left the Catholic Church for some variety of Protestant faith, with especially gruesome tales from Colombia remaining fresh in my mind these decades later. In addition, a Protestant observer could not help but conclude that rampant syncretism marked much Christianity in Latin America; formal Catholicism seemed only to overlay popular religions that retained many of the polytheistic and animistic features of pre-European contact. So, should the great numbers of Catholic adherents be counted as Christians at all?

When I turned to study the general transmission of Christianity from Europe to the Americas, the problem moved from the anecdotal to the interpretive. Latin American religion, it was clear, represented the last expression of old-world Christendom, where church and state cooperated to create a monopolistic social order. Under this regime, "deviants" (i.e., Protestants) were treated in the early twentieth century as "deviants" had been treated in sixteenth- and seventeenth-century Europe when almost all nations were officially either Catholic or Protestant. In those earlier conditions, Protestants in Catholic lands and Catholics in Protestant lands were marginalized, disadvantaged, exiled, or worse. The humanizing effects from ideologies of toleration arrived late in Latin America. From an evangelical angle, it was easy to assume that the separation of church and state, peaceful competition among religious traditions, and a clear distinction between Christianity and native religions were norms that should be found everywhere. It was, therefore, difficult to approach Latin America with any kind of empathy.

Then, when I began to read a little bit about current developments, even more complexity was added. Over the last few decades, it has become obvious that within Latin American Catholicism there now exist conservative traditionalists, progressive liberationists, much continuing folk religion, some Bible-oriented and charismatic reform, great swaths of nonparticipating indifference, and in some places growing anticlerical secularism. Just as clear are the unprecedented advances of Pentecostal-type Protestant movements in Brazil, Central America, Chile, and elsewhere. My reaction to what I first read about the latter movements was, however, also mixed. While it was encouraging to see what looked like alternatives to the stultifying sway of syncretistic Catholicism, the prominence of Protestant health-and-wealth preaching was unsettling. Even more unsettling was discovering that a few of Central America's new Protestants (specifically Ríos Montt and his henchmen in Guatemala) ranked among the world's most violently aggressive tyrants of the postwar era.

On top of all this confusion (for me) comes now Pope Francis I. In one individual we see a combination of traditional Catholic doctrine, progressive advocacy for the poor, and a willingness to criticize the type of capitalism with which earlier generations of Latin American hierarchies cooperated in order to secure their own power. Moreover, as a bishop in Argentina, Jorge Mario Bergoglio enjoyed a good relationship with evangelical Protestants who have spoken highly of his support for their prayer groups, Bible studies, and Christ-centered preaching.

Of course, Pope Francis had not yet appeared on the scene when I first offered courses on world Christianity. Yet in general, for an evangelical Protestant historian trained to analyze Christian developments in Europe and North America, the persona of the new pope only underscores the puzzles I have confronted in the contemporary world history of Christianity. The pedagogical consequence of that confusion was a syllabus where treatment of Latin America slid to the end of the semester and received much sketchier treatment than given to Africa, China, India, or even Oceania.

Thankfully, however, help was at hand to assist me in those early teaching efforts and to remain a source of great encouragement—intellectually, personally, and spiritually—right to the present.

❖

That help came in the person of John Jauchen, the founder and director of a mission called Help for Christian Nationals. For several decades this organization has been working to support church builders, evangelists, cell-group leaders, family counselors, and lay educators in several parts of the world.

We began our friendship almost half a century ago on the Wheaton College basketball team (as a freshman John was tall, angular, not particularly graceful, and not quite as good as I was; by the midpoint of our sophomore year John was a little taller, still angular and still not particularly graceful, but he had clearly passed me by). We enjoyed a year as roommates, endured many road trips with the team, and then went our separate ways.

For several years after college I appreciated opportunities for casual contact that kept me informed about his marriage to Mary Joiner (who I knew was from good Iowa stock), the birth of their children, his time playing basketball with Overseas Crusades' Sports Ambassadors, and then the beginning of missionary service in Colombia. I was glad to learn about the start-up of Help for Christian Nationals in 1982, but more because he was a valued longtime friend than for any other reason. Only later, when starting to read Andrew Walls and beginning to think about the different forms assumed by contemporary Christian movements, did I realize that my old teammate could also become my new teacher.

The teaching took place when John agreed to visit the early renditions of my world Christianity course as a guest lecturer. Early on his appearance amounted to yet another expedient designed to help me fill up a full semester, but right from the start his lectures also became a highlight of the semester in their own right. My idea in asking John to provide this instruction was for him not only to share his personal story with the class but also to provide practical guidance for any students who were considering similar missionary vocations. These goals were more than met, but they came with a bonus: a wealth of well-considered insights on the trajectory, contexts, advances, struggles, and day-to-day character of ordinary Christian existence in various regions of Latin America (and also in the Philippines where he had visited on many occasions). In other words, John provided ground-level instruction about many of the same questions, factors, and historical situations that I was trying to treat from a bird's-eye vantage point.

In his lectures, John introduced the goals of his mission, which include educational and other support for a number of Christian workers in several parts of the world. But then he took more time to explain his particular calling within the general structure. That calling involves the planning and direction of short seminars (usually three days in length) for ordinary, often newly converted or newly revived Christian workers. The seminar provides basic instruction for using the Scriptures to prepare sermons or Bible studies. It ends with students receiving, for a small fee, their own study Bibles, sometimes the first Scriptures participants have owned. John has carried out these seminars not only in many Latin American countries but also in India and extensively in the Philippines. They are always conducted in partnership with local and regional Christian leaders.

That content was what I had anticipated when asking John to take part in the classes. What I had not anticipated was the informed historical introductions he also provided about the recent history of Christianity in individual countries. Usually John singled out the Philippines and Nicaragua for that special attention. The result was detailed, firsthand reports on places in the world where Protestant-type groups were burgeoning, where some historical strains with the dominant Catholic population remained, and where local contingencies exerted a major impact on the course of development. In the Philippines contingencies included church leaders being attacked by Communist insurgents and the country's connections to Asian economic growth; in Nicaragua contingencies included hurricanes, dictatorship, civil war, and more.

In his lectures, John ably included references to material I had tried to cover: the economic and missionary ventures stimulated by the end of the Second World War, the worldwide impact of the Second Vatican Council, the mobilization of evangelicals represented by the 1974 Lausanne Congress on World Evangelization, and the fall of communism in the late 1980s. He also reminded students that Western missionary efforts had been greatly inspired by the publicity given to sacrificial service, like the five young missionaries killed by Waorani tribesmen in the Ecuadorian jungle in 1954. (The latter was an especially meaningful reference at Wheaton where three of these men had attended college and where several landmarks on campus were named in their honor.)

Mostly, however, he concentrated on the Christian vitality he had witnessed among men, women, and young people drawn from what economists would call the middle and lower classes. He would first sketch main developments in the Philippines and Nicaragua but then turn to assessments.

A chief concern was always to explain the rapid increases he witnessed in Protestant-type groups. A preliminary consideration was their tremendous diversity: churches and cell groups arose in many different ways—some from the work of long-term missionaries, others sparked by newer Pentecostal missionaries coming from outside the country, and even more arising from an extraordinary range of local leaders who were charismatic in both senses of the term (natural ability and Spirit empowerment). John then explained the common factors he saw in many situations. There has been a strong reaction against historical Roman Catholicism perceived in terms of its "idolatry." Straightforward theology that focuses on the saving work of Christ is ubiquitous. Strong local leaders relish the empowerment offered by the chance to form and guide congregations. There is zealous worship, signs and wonders (especially physical healing), positive affirmation of life in the world (often as a gospel of health and wealth), and an increasing number of cell groups with a multitude of new Christian leaders.

John then spotlighted the main reasons he saw for the rapid growth of Protestant-type groups. Many seemed to respond to the inability of traditional Catholic structures to meet pressures of globalization leading to economic stress, urban overcrowding, and especially family disintegration. In this vacuum, evangelical cell groups provided a new kind of family for spiritual and community support. Participation in religion that demanded the exercise of responsibility often fueled aspirations for social improvement in other areas. From perhaps a higher angle, strong commitment to prayer, gospel preaching, exhortation, evangelism, and community support offered directly spiritual reasons for revival, reform, and renewal.

John's ability to enliven these generalizations with specific examples from his own experience kept all of us on the edge of our seats. Often he would begin his lectures by recounting the great impact on his own life of a veteran pastor in Colombia who sold his household furniture in order to provide a new sound system that could reach interested people standing outside his church but who were hesitant about entering a Protestant building. Just as moving was his story of a Filipino pastor friend who paid with his life for maintaining a Christian witness—guerrillas carved an anti-Christian slogan into his flesh when they discarded his murdered body.

This next incident happened several years later, but it reflected the eagerness of the people who attend the seminars on biblical preaching. John was with a missionary colleague in Santiago, Chile, conducting a well-attended gathering when on the evening of February 27, 2010, a massive earthquake struck the region. John and his friend were unhurt in their hotel but naturally shaken and wondering what their next steps should be, when early the next morning students from the seminar showed up to ask them why they had delayed in arriving for the last day of their seminar, the day when participants were to receive their very own copies of the Scriptures. These students were not going to let a mere earthquake frustrate the desire for deeper biblical faith.

The riveting character of these incidents made my students listen carefully when John specified what he saw as major trends in the expansion of evangelical and Pentecostal Christianity around the world. He wanted them to realize not only that many opportunities still existed for missionaries from the developed world, but also that leadership of local churches was now firmly in the hands of locals themselves. The church planters, Bible teachers, and pastors he met were passionate, on duty all the time, mostly untrained and untooled, often uncompensated, materially poor but spiritually rich. They lived in social contexts that experienced what he called "continual disintegration of traditional belief systems." They seldom enjoyed up-to-date technology for evangelism and education (though cell phones had become ubiquitous). They suffered considerably from family strain, sometimes from the intensity of their religious commitments, but more often from desperate economic need.

For my classes, John usually stepped back to assess the challenges facing the great tide of active new believers: in Nicaragua, Pentecostal-type churches with 1 to 2 percent of the population in 1970 had 20 percent of the population by early in the twenty-first century; in the Philippines, too, they had strong but somewhat less-dramatic increases. Those challenges include intense fragmentation within almost all Protestant groups as well as lingering tensions with the Catholic heritage; difficulty in reaching local elites as well as the poorest of the poor; an urgent need to train leaders; the necessity of pushing beyond superficial expressions of the faith; the need to combat moral legalism and to promote a concern for missionary service; the pressing demand to meet ever-present economic needs; and the growing problem of preserving the results of evangelism, with larger numbers of *former* evangelicals constituting a new phenomenon in this part of the world.

His reflections on the Catholic heritage of the Philippines and Latin America were reserved and nuanced. In just the years he was lecturing to my classes, he had seen more signs in Catholic circles of social renewal, but had seen even greater interest in charismatic and biblical expressions of the faith. He also spoke of the rapidity of change: from high levels of Catholic-Protestant tension just a short time ago to the (occasional) presence of Catholic lay leaders, and even priests, at their Bible-training seminars now.

John's thorough discussions culminated in a strongly spiritual message. Without trying to link specific circumstances with specific results, he nonetheless concluded that the Holy Spirit worked actively through modern circumstances, drawing people to Christ and empowering them to live lives of faithful holiness. Although he was reluctant to draw attention to the efforts of Help for Christian Nationals, it was obvious to all of us that the Bible-training seminars were providing important scriptural ballast for those who took part.

As an example of what he was able to communicate to our class, John has given me permission to quote from a letter he sent to friends of his mission in February 2002, which he wrote on site during a visit to the south end of Lima, Peru. The mission was undertaken in cooperation with his long-standing coworker Phil Train, who had made the contacts in that area:

> When we arrive at Noah's Ark Baptist Church, the biggest church building in the area, 185 people are already squeezed into this small tin-roofed chapel. Pastors have arrived early this morning, excited and ready to begin. They believe, without a doubt, that God has selected them for this event. They feel that God brought me from America. And they have the quiet conviction that God is here. That is what matters most to them. Though their material possessions are few, and they are not known beyond these limited square miles of south Lima, they are

someone "special" because they have been born into an eternal family that today encircles the globe. Their aim for these three days is to better their pastoral skills so that they can more effectively represent Jesus Christ to their own churches and to their neighborhoods.

The church where we meet is in the heart of Villa Salvador, one of the many "joven barrios" (new neighborhoods) on this south end of Lima. No one knows for sure how many people live in the "southern cone." Most say it is between 4 and 6 million people. New families arrive each day from rural areas, seeking jobs and a better life. Quickly they discover city life is not what had been expected. Most of these barrios have no running water, no sanitation, no paved streets, and are ruled at night by gangs of teenagers that roam the streets. The new immigrants quickly become unwelcome squatters. Their eyes reflect a hopeless situation. Most live only to survive another day. . . .

On our last day together a humble pastor hands me a note of gratitude with that well-known verse from the books of Romans: "How beautiful are the feet of those who bring good news!" His intent was to encourage and thank me for coming. But I knew on this occasion that verse was *not* about me! I looked at those dusty black shoes of that Peruvian man and I saw how beautiful they must be to the people he touches each day. They were carriers of that hope so longed for. Those black shoes had walked where I will never be able to walk. I will never read those words of Paul again, without thinking of that pastor and all the others who minister so tirelessly each day in Barrio Villa Salvador of Lima, Peru.

John Jauchen's lectures did not answer all possible questions about Christian developments even in the countries he visited most often. They did, however, draw all of us a little closer to some of the day-to-day realities that monographs and articles (however perceptive) cannot convey. For me, those lectures gave bare chronicles and academic preoccupations an infusion of life, purpose, and spiritual gravity.

❖15❖

Looking South:
Academic Insights

John Jauchen's timely assistance began what was for me the especially difficult task of incorporating the recent history of Latin American Christianity into a broader story. Soon, however, I was grateful to discover other resources that from other angles supplemented John's personal instruction. Some of that assistance came from an author whose work I already knew but had not considered for this part of the world, and some from writers who were entirely new.

❖

Early on in teaching conventional church history courses, I had discovered sociologist David Martin's *A General Theory of Secularization*, a book published in the late 1970s that made sense out of a great deal of the European and North American past.[1] In the summary of his insights that I regularly repeated to classes, I simplified Martin's much fuller presentation like this: the shape of a society

1. David Martin, *A General Theory of Secularization* (New York: Harper & Row, 1978).

147

when it was comprehensively Christian will strongly influence the way secularization takes hold when Christianity begins to fade. Again with much simplification of Martin's rich account, I passed on to students an ordering of national histories arranged along a spectrum from authoritarian (or hegemonic) to liberal (or loosey-goosey).

At the authoritarian end was Russian caesaropapism where the czar, aspiring to exert all power, ran the Orthodox Church as one part of his comprehensive regime—giving way to a Communist government that, again aspiring to be all-powerful, tried to eliminate the Orthodox Church as a dangerous rival to its comprehensive authority.

Then came France: from a powerful Catholic establishment operating in league with absolute monarchs—moving to a powerful anticlerical secularism in an all-out, but usually not violent, struggle against the lingering authority of church and tradition.

Next were the German-speaking lands: from strong church-state unions, but divided among Catholic and Protestant regimes, and with much open space for representatives of a more secular Enlightenment—moving to continuing church-state connections, but balancing Protestant and Catholic interests alongside an influential range of ideas and institutions that did not have much use for Christianity.

Then Britain: a relatively mild church-state establishment with, eventually, considerable room for Dissenting Protestants—giving way to a largely secular culture that nonetheless retained its church-state establishment and offered free-church Protestants and (eventually) Catholics, Jews, and others space to do what they could without much official interference.

And finally the United States with a free market of religion where churches and Christian agencies, through much of the nineteenth century, organized voluntarily into an informal Christian civilization—giving way to a much more secular America but where free market practices allowed many religious groups to retain influence without seeming to worry much about the secularization of law, media, entertainment, and most of political life.

Martin, in other words, made big-picture sense out of the general sweep of the Western history of Christianity. Ah, but why not also Latin America? By the time that penny dropped, Martin had published two more outstanding books that helped to explain the immense recent changes in Latin American economic life, culture, society—and religion.[2]

David Martin's type of sociology is not the wannabe-scientific variety where human activities, interests, and convictions are quantified and then locked into tight formulas. His work stands, rather, alongside books by Edwards Shils, Robert Bellah, Robert Wuthnow, and Peter Berger—social scientists who sometimes use a lot of factual data but always for the purpose of offering flexible human interpretations of the subjects they study. Martin's upbringing in England included participation in local Methodist churches; he won his reputation as a sociologist of religion during a long career at the London School of Economics; he later became an ordained Anglican; and, unusually for modern sociologists, he has not backed away from inserting theological interpretations into at least some of his influential books and articles.

For Latin America, Martin's help was comprehensive. It aided me in understanding the long enduring Catholic past as well as recent changes connected with the rapid expansion of mostly Pentecostal Protestantism. For the earlier history he showed why it was necessary to view Latin American Catholicism as a cultural system even more than as an expression of theology or church life. That culture represented an organization and style of life even more than a message; it was different from Protestantism in organic conceptions even more than in beliefs. As Martin put it, "The roots of Catholicism . . . lie in territory, birthright membership, the organic frame, communal obligation, and peoplehood. That means that it places a sacred canopy over the average and the religiously relaxed, and lacks a defined and incisive edge." The difficulties that all styles of Protestantism long experienced in Latin America arose because "Catholicism can never be at its ease with the fissiparous dynamism of untutored religious entrepreneurship."[3]

2. David Martin, *Tongues of Fire: The Explosion of Pentecostalism in Latin America* (Cambridge, MA: Blackwell, 1990); *Pentecostalism: The World Their Parish* (Malden, MA: Blackwell, 2002).
3. Martin, *Pentecostalism*, 17.

Martin does not reduce either traditional Catholicism or modern Latin American Pentecostalism to supposedly more basic structural realities. Yet as with his assessment of secularization, he can show that certain Christian expressions align more easily with some social shapes, forces, and authorities than with others.

Thus, for the postwar history of Latin America, Martin sees the hurricane force of economic globalization as a crucial influence. The economic disparities unleashed by that force have stimulated violent revolutionary movements from both the Left and the Right. But Martin insists that globalization stimulated, facilitated, and developed in conjunction with a number of other forces, among which Pentecostal Christianity has been one of the most important.

Here is Martin's logic, which in broad theoretical terms matches very well what John Jauchen taught me from his observations on the ground: Latin America has witnessed powerful ruptures—everywhere economic, sometimes connected with revolutionary violence, often resulting from natural disasters like hurricanes or earthquakes. These ruptures have had the effect of detaching huge populations, especially the poor and dispossessed, from historical practices, authorities, obligations, and conventions. Both traditional Catholicism and new-wave Pentecostalism can be viewed as responding to these ruptures, but in strikingly different ways: "The Catholic Church has assimilated many cultural traits . . . , but it has done so as an absorbent system, whereas Pentecostalism is a prolific set of burgeoning affinities, constituted by recognition of kind."[4] In other words, Martin suggests that Pentecostalism flourishes as a result of personal choices by people in new situations, while Catholicism tries to meet new situations with resources for those who have grown up in the church.

The reasoning that Martin once applied to the history of Western Christianity he has now applied to the history of Christianity outside of the West. He concludes that "what moves people on the move and turns their atomized being into a corporate movement is a repertoire of religious images corresponding to their circumstance." By referring to both direct encounter with the God of Pentecostal worship

4. Ibid., 170.

and the structure that Pentecostal conversion often brings to daily life, Martin can explain "that millions on the move know themselves to be released from ascribed categories and indelible markers into a dangerous and bewildering open-endedness which has been made meaningful and purposeful by a discipline that offers a destination."[5]

In Martin's account, Europe witnesses only small-scale Pentecostal movements because the relative numbers destabilized by economic modernization are small. North America witnesses some vigorous Pentecostal movements, but alongside a wide variety of other Protestant activities (he points out that North America is the only part of the world that has witnessed significant Protestant advances that are not Pentecostal). In Latin America, by contrast, once the long-standing dominant culture has been disturbed, Pentecostal forms of Christianity offer the immediate presence of God and powerful guides for individuals who are able to put their lives together voluntarily. Martin's emphasis on "forms of Pentecostalism" is also insightful since what he calls "choice" churches, as opposed to traditional "place" churches, can appear in many forms—as in Brazil where huge new denominations like the Universal Church of the Kingdom of God flourish alongside micro or house-based assemblies with no visible hierarchies or connections.

Martin's observations have been of great help in trying to fit Latin America into the world Christian picture, especially his (as John Stackhouse once phrased it in an insightful profile) "particular, and often bracing, observations that bring clarity to what was heretofore only dimly seen."[6] Significantly, those observations include a specifically Christian overlay that makes theological sense out of what he describes sociologically. So, for example, on what often looks like the completely unregulated use of Scripture by nascent Pentecostal movements, Martin concedes that "where there are as many interpretations as there are readers, and the Spirit is unbounded," we seem to be viewing one of the traditional weaknesses of Protestantism. Yet

5. Ibid., 168.
6. John G. Stackhouse Jr., "David Martin: Sociologist as Servant of the Church," *Books & Culture*, May/June 2004, 39.

"in today's world," as he describes it, "when the niches and needs are so varied, Pentecostalism works by constant adjustment on the ground."[7] Among his last words on the subject of Pentecostalism, we return again to the major themes that have so fruitfully informed the work of Andrew Walls, Lamin Sanneh, and other leading interpreters of recent history: Christianity, at the end of the day, is not a program but "a narrative of transformations and transfigurations."[8]

A request in 2007 to write an essay-review of four books on the history of Christianity in Latin America provided an opportunity to synthesize what I had been taught by my friend John Jauchen and my book-mentor David Martin. Each of the books was intriguing in itself, but even more intriguing was what I took to be the commonalities they described.[9] Whether my effort to treat them together was correct, students have been doomed to hear variations of what follows whenever this area of the world arrives on the syllabus.

Those of us who have been trained as students of Western Christian or North American religious history must make a major intellectual adjustment when turning south. Where the religious lives of precontact First Peoples throughout the Western Hemisphere bore some similarities of cult and cosmology among themselves, once European settlement began, a sharp divide separated developments in what became the United States and Canada from what became the countries of Mexico and southwards. To be sure, the religion of all European settlements came out of the cauldron of sixteenth-century Reformation and Counter-Reformation conflict and so shared a certain

7. Martin, *Pentecostalism*, 170.

8. Ibid., 176.

9. The books were Osvaldo F. Pardo, *The Origins of Mexican Catholicism: Nahua Rituals and Christian Sacraments in Sixteenth-Century Mexico* (Ann Arbor: University of Michigan Press, 2004); José de Acosta, *Natural and Moral History of the Indies*, ed. Jane E. Mangan, trans. Frances López-Morillas, intro. Walter D. Mignolo (Durham, NC: Duke University Press, 2002); Matthew Butler, *Popular Piety and Political Identity in Mexico's Cristero Rebellion: Michoacán, 1927–1929* (New York: Oxford University Press, 2004); and Rebecca J. Lester, *Jesus in Our Wombs: Embodying Modernity in a Mexican Convent* (Berkeley: University of California Press, 2005).

agenda about which to violently disagree. In addition, the colonization of New France (later Quebec) by leaders advocating ideals of the Catholic Reformation meant that one corner of North America would, in some particulars, resemble what other representatives of Catholic reform were trying to establish in Latin America. But even with that resemblance, the religion of seventeenth-century Catholic France promoted a spirituality, an approach to native peoples, and attitudes toward church-state connections much closer to the religion of the British and Dutch Protestant colonies than was being planted in the Spanish and Portuguese Catholic colonies.

North America, in the main, would be Protestant, of a strongly Dissenting influence, and it would rely largely on voluntary organization; Latin America was Catholic and of a strongly integralist hue that strove toward an ideal of social-cultural unity. North American colonists mostly wiped out or isolated native populations as they went about replanting European Christianity; Spanish and Portuguese colonies in Latin America largely absorbed the native populations and tolerated a syncretism of native religions and European Christianity. North American religion accepted (relatively quickly) intra-Protestant diversity and showed how lay religious initiative could create the mediating institutions of civil society; Latin America witnessed a stronger Catholic homogeneity than anywhere else in the world during the early modern period and (for its first centuries) a social order organized by crown and cross from the top down. North America moved rapidly, if also with considerable friction, toward what became the separation of church and state; in Latin America the early arrangement whereby the Spanish and Portuguese monarchs received nearly carte blanche to organize the church (called Patronato or Padroado Real) encouraged much more authoritarian assumptions about connections between church and state. In North America the usual Christian leaders were married pastors exerting limited authority in settled communities with many other centers of cultural power; in Latin America celibate leaders of religious orders exercising broad powers over native and mixed European-Indian communities competed with viceroys and colonial officials for cultural power. Perhaps most importantly, North American religious history has always been marked by forces of Christianity and forces of political liberalism moving in roughly the same direction (though more obviously in the Thirteen Colonies/United States than in British North America/Canada); in Latin America the forces of Christianity and political liberalism have been mostly opposed.

It is obviously dangerous to generalize about a mythical unified Latin American religious world. Yet while not denying a great deal of diversity, it is still the case that Latin American religious history reveals striking contrasts to North American religious history. The sharpest of these contrasts can perhaps be stated in two complementary ways.

Latin American Christianity seems to be a religion of the body as contrasted to a North American Christianity understood as a religion of the mind. Of course, Latin American believers have engaged the intellect, and North American believers have embodied their faith. But throughout Latin America, the physicality of religion seems everywhere in the foreground—from sixteenth-century missionaries adapting European sacramental rites to Native American life-stage rituals to Catholics in Mexico's Cristero War (1926–29) risking their lives by removing crucifixes from sequestered church buildings and contemporary nuns in thriving convents devoting significant moments of each day to contemplating the Eucharist as preparation for service in the world. Highlights of North American Christian history, by contrast, are sermons (think Jonathan Edwards), influential publications (think William Lloyd Garrison or *The Late Great Planet Earth*), and consent or rejection of verbal appeals for conversion. The contrast is far from absolute, but it is there.

Similar is a contrast between religion as an institutional given of community life and religion as a chosen vehicle for creating civil society. Personal identity in traditional Latin American religion certainly demanded effort, but that effort involved accepting what had been handed down. In North America the effort so often required for defining personal identity meant grasping open possibilities. In Latin American peoples' religion, power was usually exerted to confirm authority and strengthen local community; in North American peoples' religion, power was more often exerted to resist authority and protect local community. Latin American traditional Catholicism was once a religion that inspired community cohesion; still today it can nerve traditional communities to contest disruptive forces coming from the outside. North America's characteristic forms of Protestantism have been religions that create fissures within community or that nerve self-selected communities to combat other self-selected American communities. In both, the force of religion for persons is inextricably related to the force of religion for communities, but the relationship is different, and the differences are rooted in strikingly contrasting histories.

❖

From both John Jauchen and David Martin, I have been instructed in what has happened when traditional Latin cultures confront the upsets of rapid population growth and economic globalization. By heeding John Jauchen and reading David Martin, I have better understood traditional Catholicism, other forces that are roiling the region, and the stakes for both traditional and new forms of Christian faith.

❖ 16 ❖

China Watching

Asia posed a different sort of challenge. How was it possible to grasp even the barest historical outline for a region with half the world's population, with Christian movements both very old (the Thomas Christians of India) and very new (neo-Pentecostalism in India, Korea, China, and elsewhere), with some areas where Western missionary influence remains strong and some where it never existed, and with a huge diversity of friendly, unfriendly, and neutral political contexts? As with so much of what I have learned about other parts of the world, teachers were the key. Sometimes the teaching came through books and articles, sometimes from personal connections, but—most memorably—it came when things to read and instruction from friends were intertwined.

For India, it has been a privilege to know Bob Frykenberg even before I realized I would be interested in world Christianity. Once that interest awakened, I benefited tremendously from Bob's occasional personal guidance as well as from the wealth of insightful writing produced by this son of Scandinavian-American missionaries and veteran University of Wisconsin professor.[1] In addition, one of the most riveting books I encountered when flailing about for early help in preparing lectures turns out to have come from a scholar whom Bob Frykenberg mentored. The scholar is Susan Billington Harper; her book, *In the Shadow of the Mahatma: Bishop V. S. Azariah and the Travails of Christianity in British India* (Eerdmans, 2000), portrays one of the most consequential, as well as the most attractive, Christian leaders from anywhere in the world during the first half of the twentieth century.

For Korea, I received a different kind of help from my Wheaton College colleague, S. Steve Kang. Steve, who has gone on to teach at Gordon-Conwell Theological Seminary, several times provided guest lectures for my Wheaton course that expertly outlined the history of Christianity in modern Korea. He has been particularly helpful in pointing out the significant ways in which that history contrasts with what occurred elsewhere in the Far East. For example, in Korea, Christianity in general and missionary-sponsored translation of the Scriptures into the local vernacular were perceived from the outset as a positive, modernizing, and anticolonial force rather than as an unwanted intrusion from the imperialistic West.

In Japan, the contrasts with other Asian countries are striking. For that history, I learned a great deal from the research papers of several students, especially Jo Ann Nishimoto and Judd Birdsall, and even more from the writings of and personal conversations with my Wheaton history department colleague Genzo Yamamoto. They instructed me in the moving history of Japan's sixteenth-century encounter with Catholicism and in the complex modern developments that help explain why Christian faith has been enduringly significant but never particularly popular in the Land of the Rising Sun.

China, however, has been the great puzzle. I remember distinctly several missionary conferences in Cedar Rapids from the 1950s where we received an unmistakable message. Perhaps it was delivered by a veteran missionary expelled from the People's Republic, or maybe

---

1. As examples, Robert Eric Frykenberg, *Christianity in India from Beginnings to the Present* (New York: Oxford University Press, 2008); and editor with Judith M. Brown, *Christians, Cultural Interactions, and India's Religious Traditions* (Grand Rapids: Eerdmans, 2002).

only from reports from that part of the world, but the message was loud and clear: China had been "lost to the gospel."

Yet by the late 1980s when China had charged back into the world economy and I had begun to think about Christianity around the globe, the gospel there seemed anything but lost. Reports proliferated about relaxed government attitudes toward the Three Self Patriotic Movement (officially registered churches), about an exploding welter of what were often referred to as "underground churches," and about the unexpected eagerness of Chinese academics to attend lectures on Christian topics presented by visiting scholars from the West. For anyone paying even partial attention, here seemed to be a conundrum indeed. What is the historical explanation for what Lamin Sanneh has written as perhaps the best short account of the history of Christianity in China immediately after Mao Zedong's reign: "As the flood receded, the rock appeared"?[2]

Thankfully, ready to hand was a personal authority to guide me and many others through the thicket of perplexing questions occasioned by modern Chinese developments. Daniel Bays had been drawn into the network of historians associated with the Institute for the Study of American Evangelicals (ISAE) through his friendship with Grant Wacker and Edith Blumhofer, two of that network's mainstays. Since organization for the ISAE was always a matter of Flexible Casual, no one raised an eyebrow when this veteran China scholar joined meetings and conferences run by and for students of North American Christianity. Dan not only fit right in but also eventually made a major contribution to one of the institute's most creative investigations in American history. With Grant Wacker he directed a project exploring the impact that missionary service abroad exerted on developments in the United States.[3] Just as important, he became a source from whom his more provincial friends and colleagues could learn a great deal about matters far from home.

2. Lamin Sanneh, *Disciples of All Nations: Pillars of World Christianity* (New York: Oxford University Press, 2008), 255.

3. Daniel Bays and Grant Wacker, eds., *The Foreign Missionary Enterprise at Home: Explorations in North American Cultural History* (Tuscaloosa: University of Alabama Press, 2003).

So it was that from his position first in the University of Kansas history department and then as a colleague of Joel Carpenter at Calvin College, Dan offered a kind of loosely organized traveling seminar on one of the most fascinating chapters in the entire history of Christianity. When Dan and his wife, Jan, returned from their frequent trips to Hong Kong or the Mainland, they brought back well-considered, firsthand accounts of religion on the ground. The many revealing contacts established through Jan's wide-ranging musical abilities, along with experiences reported by both American and Chinese students, added texture. Dan was particularly helpful as he urged judicious caution in assessing the breathless reports of hasty journalists. Yes, numbers of Christian believers were growing very fast, but not as fast as some visitors claimed. Yes, persecution remained very real in some parts of China, but was almost entirely absent in others. Yes, renewed contacts with the West had a real impact, but they were not nearly as influential as the paths that Chinese believers were carving out for themselves. The questions with which we bombarded Dan and Jan they answered carefully, informatively, and with extraordinary sensitivity. From them we learned much about the singular features of China's regional subcultures, the pervasive concern of the government for overarching control, the complex connections between economic freedom and religious possibilities, and the many varieties of Christian faith apparent early in the twenty-first century.

Dan also provided authoritative guidance as to what was worth reading and what could be set aside for those of us who, while remaining at home, still sought reliable accounts. Thanks to this advice, I was steered away from a few books that had been trumpeted in the media and guided to much more reliable volumes by scholars such as Ryan Dunch, Philip Wickeri, Alvin Austin, Xi Lian, and others.

Over time, it also dawned on me that this walking encyclopedia had also written and edited unusually helpful materials of his own. From a number of his earlier books and articles, and then from the luminous pages of his *A New History of Christianity in China* (Wiley-Blackwell, 2012), I received a wealth of insight that informs everything I now try to teach, lecture, or write about this corner of the world.

The insights include an awareness that China's ancient Christian history, dating back to Nestorian missionaries from the Middle East in the seventh century, retains an unusual resonance for a contemporary society deeply anxious about its past, its future, and the connections between its past and present. Again, Dan early on pointed out the significance of China-guided indigenous Christian movements, arising very early in the twentieth century but hidden from Western eyes by concentration on missionaries. Such movements turned out to be the key to the faith's survival and even expansion in the years of all-out Communist opposition. He also explained why official attitudes to religion paralleled the treatment of all social organizations: so long as the absolute control of centralized power could be maintained, associations (including churches) have come to enjoy a great deal of free space; when, however, that power is even apparently threatened (as with the Falun Gong), authorities are almost certain to crack down hard.

This kind of instruction allowed me to make sense of a curious incident that had taken place several years before. Sometime in the late 1990s, Wheaton College entertained a body of visiting Chinese business and governmental leaders for a day of lectures introducing them to Christian expressions in the United States. My assignment was to sketch the history of religious movements, which I did by emphasizing how churches had adapted to the free-form, entrepreneurial, and democratic culture that developed in the United States after the American Revolution. When it came time for questions from the floor, one of the visitors asked, "But who is in charge of religious life in the United States?" I replied that, well, no one exactly; religion is directed mostly from below by leaders who are able to maintain or attract a following. The next question: "But, really, who is in charge?" Instead of repeating what I had just said, I asked our expert translator how the idea of "civil society" (self-guided organizational culture) could be rendered into Chinese. He replied, in effect, that the Chinese do not have such a phrase. This exchange seemed only an eccentric curiosity until Dan Bays explained the historical Chinese fixation on the need for an all-comprehending social order guided from the top down.

❖

Thanks to Dan, his writing, and other authoritative sources to which he has pointed, I now very much look forward to the part of my class that deals with China. It has even become challenging to limit treatment of so much fascinating material.

A wealth of crucial incidents fairly calls out for sustained assessments. What, for example, should be made of the early Nestorian mission, and even more of the extensive period of Catholic missionary activity under the leadership of great scholar-teachers like Matteo Ricci that lasted from the late sixteenth century into the early eighteenth? Both of those episodes showed not only how well Christianity could adapt to a situation beyond Christendom but also how fragile the planting of Christianity could be when no official government or social support existed.

Then the entire nineteenth century is filled with a tumult of dramatic developments. Renewed efforts by Catholic missionaries, as well as pioneering efforts by Protestants—like Robert Morrison in Guanzhou or the plebian recruits who staffed the China Inland Mission that Hudson Taylor founded—demonstrated considerable sympathy for aspects of Chinese society that Westerners interested only in trade ignored. By the end of the century missionaries like James Legge and Timothy Richard went even further in actively promoting study of classical Chinese culture and trying to explain Christianity in indigenous Chinese terms. From the other side of the moral register, the Opium Wars of 1839–42 found many missionaries cooperating with the British East India Company as it used armed force to open China to the narcotics trade—a complicity in aggression that remains alive to this day as a warning to some Chinese against the perils of Western "imperialist religion." The terrible Taiping Rebellion of the mid-nineteenth century, with its millions of lost lives, had enough connection to Christian teaching, however misunderstood, to further complicate the place of Christianity in Chinese society. At the same time when Legge and Richard were showing the essential compatibility of nonimperialist Christianity with Chinese cultural values, the Boxer Rebellion of 1900 sparked resistance to everything coming from the

West. Christian circles in Europe and North America mourned the death of missionaries attacked by the Boxers (the "League of Righteous Fists"), but the ones who suffered in much greater numbers were Chinese believers.

The twentieth century, which began with the Boxer Rebellion, experienced a continuous series of momentous events in which local Christians and missionaries were almost always fully active participants. They include the 1911 Revolution, which established the Republic of China and was guided by the baptized Christian Sun Yat-sen; the popular protests of 1919 and 1922 that attacked Western influence, including missionaries; the development of Chinese higher education that was spurred by missionary initiatives and directed in substantial part by a whole corps of Chinese Christian academics; the bitter conflict between Nationalists under Chiang Kai-Shek and Communists under Mao Zedong that flared in the 1930s, receded as the Chinese rallied to oppose the Japanese invasion later in that decade, then burst out with renewed force until the triumph of the Communists in 1949; then the violent unfolding of Mao's regime that included the Great Leap Forward (1958–60) and the Great Proletarian Revolution (1966–76) that took direct aim at any vestige of Western influence, including the churches.

Through this brutal century that witnessed so many levels of conflict, the focus of most Western observers remained on the missionaries. Thus, it was only natural that when the Communist regime expelled them in the early 1950s, commentary in North America and Europe resounded with the words I had heard in Cedar Rapids. Only after the relaxations following Mao's death in 1976 did outsiders begin to see the central Christian story that had been developing for over a century. That story concerned the Chinese who for their own purposes and with their own resources had been demonstrating the capacity of the faith to become a distinctly Chinese religion.

Historically considered—and in hindsight, with the assistance of the careful research undertaken by scholars like Daniel Bays—it is possible to outline the recent history of Christianity as a striking paradox. In this picture, Mao Zedong counts as one of the most significant figures in modern Christian history—not because of what he tried to do but because of what happened inadvertently through his actions. Thus, Mao attacked Confucian culture as one of the "olds" that the Communist regime would replace with his own Thought; in so doing he loosened the grip of this conceptual system and made it possible for the Chinese to think about alternative ways of construing the world. Then, by expelling all Western missionaries, Mao also decisively broke the image of Christianity in China as a mere appendage of Western religious movements. Both the Three Self Patriotic Church that took shape under Communist control and the unregistered churches that stayed out of the Three Self Movement were, whatever else anyone might say about them, obviously Chinese. But then the disasters of Mao's own regime—with millions imprisoned, starved, killed, or displaced—demonstrated the inability of his form of communism to satisfy social or personal human needs. The result (once Mao's successors loosened their tight grip in order to attempt economic liberation) was much greater opportunity for other forms of self-guided organization. In that environment, a number of different forms of Christian faith emerged out of the background, where they had bided time during the period of intense persecution. These different forms have continued to expand with great diversity to the present. But now, in contrast to the years before the triumph of Communist rule, they exist unquestionably as Chinese churches charting their own path.

This kind of capsule account cannot do justice to China's extraordinary recent history. I am, however, grateful to Daniel Bays and to the kind of scholarship his writing represents for making it possible even to attempt such a summary statement.

❖

If not already, Asia will almost certainly soon be the world's leader in technology, wealth creation, military might, and cultural diversity—as well as in number of people. If the Christian past is going to grow into the Christian future, what happens in Asia is of paramount importance. Moreover, in all of Asia, China offers one of the very best "laboratories" for discerning what Christianity can mean without the history of Western Christendom and without the interweaving of

religion, political authority, economic activity, and educational guidance that has marked European history since the Middle Ages and
that has prevailed in North America in democratized form. Chinese
Christians—at least partially in contrast to Africa, Latin America,
and even the South Sea Islands—face the challenge of advancing in a
mature society still deeply shaped by Confucian culture and its more
recent experience of communism. Trying to understand historical
dynamics that are so different from European and American history
(while learning about Christian churches that, to appearances, came
back from the dead) remains one of the most daunting, but also
stimulating, tasks I have ever encountered.

❖ 17 ❖

Explorations
with Pen in Hand

nce launched onto the sea of world Christianity, it was obvious that this ocean was very large. Personal guides, who
almost literally took me by the hand, remained indispensable motivators—Don Church, George Rawlyk, John Jauchen, and
Daniel Bays. Key books by Andrew Walls and a few others marked
paths leading outwards. Yet I soon discovered that vast resources
existed for charting the recent course of Christianity throughout the
world. From one angle, that realization delivered a humbling shock.
How could any single individual even begin to grasp what this rapidly
expanding plethora of reliable writings told about recent Christian
history—the regions, languages, cultures, churches, parachurches,
personalities, tragedies, triumphs, conflicts, experiments, surprises,
disappointments, spectacular events, and day-to-day realities?

Yet from another angle, the more confusion that trying to look
at the whole world created, the greater the basic simplicity of what
such an effort revealed. Jesus as Son of God was always at the center. The Scriptures provided an ever-present template. Transformed
lives—along with an almost universal recognition of falling short of

Christian ideals—showed up everywhere. The same type of struggles seemed to prevail between self-fixated religiosity and self-giving altruism, between courageous fidelity and craven hypocrisy. It was definitely *not* a matter of essential Christianity cloaked in superficial cultural varieties. Instead, it was Christianity recognizably taking shape—all the way down, with no cultural residue—in an incredibly diverse range of local expressions.

To be sure, it did take a while to appreciate the potential integrity of these myriad local experiences. Western Christians generally, and the evangelicals of my own tradition specifically, had tended to regard our own expressions of the faith as somehow uniquely normative, floating as if they were free from Western cultural development (or the particular history of American fundamentalism/evangelicalism). Consequently, it was necessary to push back against the instinct to treat *my own* Christianity as simply normative Christianity. Yet once coming to realize that the Christianity I embraced was also a local cultural expression made it easier, at least conceptually, to appreciate the development of Christianity in shapes very different from my own.

Trusting in the one God revealed as Father, Son, and Holy Spirit kept this line of thinking from descending into complete cultural relativity. But believing that the Maker of heaven and earth had become flesh (that is, deity translated into humanity) also prepared the way for expecting great diversity as the faith was repeatedly retranslated over the course of time.

To the extent that such conclusions took hold, they did so not only in the classroom but also as I was asked to write book reviews, prepare articles, and then attempt my own books. The reviews sampled the incredible range of solid writing that from the mid-twentieth century has made it possible to learn about Christianity far from home. Writing articles (that were often revised versions of lectures) provided an opportunity to explore connections and comparisons. And writing books widened the opportunity to develop a few ideas at greater length.

By personal instinct and professional vocation, I was accustomed to carrying out such explorations with pen in hand. Now these writing assignments presented a way for moving from mere wonderment at the expanding realities of world Christianity toward preliminary conclusions about what it all meant. For me, a new periodical, *Books & Culture: A Christian Review*, opened the door. InterVarsity Press, with the assistance of friends Carolyn Nystrom, Joel Scandrett, and Andy LePeau, pushed me through.

❖

Books & Culture was in some ways the *Reformed Journal* come back to life. It first appeared late in 1995 and has remained an intellectual beacon in a public landscape grown ever more contested as blog posts crowd out the kind of thoughtful journalism this magazine represents. Cooperation between complementary strands of postwar conservative Protestantism made it happen.

From one side came a number of writers, advisors, and readers who had mourned the passing of the *Reformed Journal*. Grand Rapids was their Mecca and the Christian Reformed Church an ecclesiastical home base. But having already made the move out into broader venues, many of them enlisted willingly as firm supporters of this new venture. Crucial start-up funding even came from an officer at the Pew Charitable Trusts who had longed to see something like the *Reformed Journal* reemerge. *Books & Culture*, as a tabloid-sized bimonthly, did not replicate the understated elegance of the *Reformed Journal*'s gray-on-white monthly pages. But it did sustain the effort to provide discerning, well-crafted, and occasionally wry observations on literature, history, theology, science, communications, world affairs, politics, even music and art. Although some of its articles have offered this commentary without overt religious comment, most have taken advantage of the subtitle, "a Christian review," to bring Christian evaluations into play directly. It, thus, carries on the *Reformed Journal*'s Kuyperian desire to record the sovereignty of Christ over every aspect of creation.

From another side came the practical sponsorship, journalistic expertise, intellectual encouragement, and extensive evangelical networks of Christianity Today International. Its publishers and editors had been looking for a way to add a more reflective Christian assessment of—well—"books and culture" to what they were already doing with *Christianity Today* magazine, *Leadership* magazine, and a broad stable of other periodicals. The institutional home and substantial financial commitment provided by Christianity Today resulted in a magazine with not only a tad more populism than the *Reformed Journal* but also a broader array of writers and readers.

Christianity Today contributed most directly to the success of this venture when it convinced John Wilson to give up his secure job with a California publisher to become the editor. John, an omnivorous reader with a Christian vision as deep as it is generous, was an ideal choice. He has opened the pages of *Books & Culture* to a number of writers already well known in Christian circles and often far beyond; he has recruited an even deeper cast of younger women and men who are at the stage of breaking into print; he has promoted the ideals of the magazine (judicious, nonideological, comprehensive, Christian) in his travels and correspondence with readers; and he has managed the ever-full pipeline of articles waiting to be published with as much consideration as possible for authors impatient to see their essays in print. I have been privileged to advise John on books, topics, and potential authors. He has been more than generous in soliciting articles from me, including quite a few dealing with the world history of Christianity.

So it was that *Books & Culture* became a forum where I could report on important books, think about Western church history as extended into global contexts, and explore parts of the world about which I had been ignorant. The important books included paradigm-shaping efforts by Andrew Walls (*The Missionary Movement in Christian History*) and Philip Jenkins (*The Next Christendom*). Reviews of such general treatment also show how rapidly world consciousness has come to inform these narratives. The books by Walls and Jenkins from the 1990s and early 2000s announced that a new Christian world had appeared and pointed toward how it should be studied. In my most recent essay for the magazine (November/December 2013), I could report on books that had taken up the challenge to compose generally global narratives. One was the second volume of Dale Irvin and Scott Sunquist's *History of the Christian Movement* (Orbis, 2012), which is exemplary for combining much that is familiar from previous texts with much that arises from fresh research about the non-Western world. The other was David Hempton's *The Church in the Long Eighteenth Century* (I. B. Tauris, 2011), a book of rare wisdom that interprets standard themes in Western Christian history with the whole world in view—and vice versa.

Extending Western history into the world meant looking at another kind of book. The chance to write an essay on Andrew Porter's *The Imperial Horizons of British Protestant Missions, 1880–1914* (Eerdmans, 2003) made it possible to follow an expert historian of British public life who was now studying the British Empire fully aware of the postcolonial and anti-imperial perspectives of much recent historiography. It was similar with Bruce Hoffman's *Inside Terrorism* (Columbia University Press, 1998), a book that well before 9/11 showed how the revival of militant Islam had made a fraction of the Muslim world dangerous in a context of Western secular complacency.

The appearance of *Books & Culture* was announced through a special insert in the regularly appearing July 1995 issue of *Christianity Today*. For that insert I was privileged to prepare an article that treated two of the giants of modern South African—indeed, of modern world—history. The article reviewed two recently appearing books, Peter F. Alexander's biography of Alan Paton (Oxford University Press, 1994) and the autobiography of Nelson Mandela, *Long Walk to Freedom* (Little, Brown, 1994). The hope of the new magazine was to allow sufficient space for more than brief summaries and off-the-cuff evaluations. I was thus given about eighteen hundred words, an unusually generous provision. But, of course, I had to read the books first. That reading, along with more reading for more assignments, became a way not only to encounter a larger world but also to explain why such explorations could be important. That first *Books & Culture* essay began like this:

> Two striking incidents from these estimable books intimate the depth—but also the ironies—of Christian faith in modern South Africa. Alan Paton (1903–1988) won worldwide renown when in 1948 he published *Cry, the Beloved Country*, an intensely powerful novel of inter-racial antagonism, murder, despair, and (at the end) forgiveness. When in

the 1950s and 1960s he helped guide South Africa's Liberal Party as a voice for non-violent, multi-racial reform, he was subjected to serious harassment from the South African government even as he won the support of many reformers inside and out of his country. Before he became widely known through his writing and political activities, however, Paton had served as the superintendent of a juvenile prison for non-whites at Deipkloof, south of Johannesburg. As a humane and largely successful administrator, Paton tried to promote inner direction, as well as outward conformity, in his charges. To that end in 1935 or 1936 he introduced a daily half-hour of Bible study. Not long thereafter one of the boys was accused of stealing fish from a nearby store. When Paton asked his black staff for advice, they urged him to use corporal punishment to get at the truth. But after only a few cuts of the cane, the lad sprang up and accused Paton of "crucifying me." He then called the African warder who was accusing him "Judas," the black vice-principal "Herod," and Paton "Pontius Pilate." Paton was deeply moved, apologized profusely, and let the boy go. Later the same afternoon, Paton went searching for the lad to offer his apologies again, but when he found the boy he was eating a hunk of the stolen fish.

About twenty years later, Nelson Mandela . . . was on the road. A few years earlier he had qualified as a lawyer and had established, with his partner Oliver Tambo, the first African legal office in the city of Johannesburg. Increasingly, however, Mandela was drawn toward political activism through the work of the African National Congress (ANC), a multi-racial organization that had already been in existence for nearly half a century. Now in the fall of 1955, Mandela was traveling through Natal and the Cape Province to encourage local ANC units to resist the policies of the Nationalist Government, which had come to power in 1948, the same year that Paton's novel, *Cry, the Beloved Country*, was published, and which had immediately begun transforming South Africa's hereditary racist conventions into full-scale, legal apartheid. When Mandela arrived in Cape Town, he was welcomed into the home of the Rev. Walter Teka, pastor of a Wesleyan church. Mandela's guides for much of his stay were Johnson Ngwevela and Greenwood Ngotyana, who were Communists as well as members of the ANC. The first Sunday of Mandela's visit he arose with the expectation of making another foray into the countryside, but was surprised to learn that all ANC business was called off. Why? The Communists

Ngwevela and Ngotyana were also ardent Wesleyans who kept the Sabbath strictly. As Mandela sums up the episode: "I protested, but to no avail. Communism and Christianity, at least in Africa, were not mutually exclusive."

These incidents illustrate the treasures to be found in the two books, which tell us not only about Paton and Mandela, but also about the volatile mix of religion and society in an intensely Christian, but also intensely divided, region of the world.

A few years later, John Wilson gave me the opportunity to write at similar length about a memorable conference convened in this same South Africa. The meeting took place in July 2001 at the Hammanskraal retreat center maintained north of Johannesburg by the University of Pretoria. It was organized by the directors of a project called Currents in World Christianity: Brian Stanley from Britain, J. W. Hofmeyr from South Africa, and Mark Hutchinson from Australia. The meeting entailed a great deal of personal satisfaction for Maggie, our son Robert, and myself—not just from visiting South Africa but also from the chance to meet the family of Dean Venables, who would wed our daughter, Mary, later that fall. The meeting itself was revelatory for displaying a full range of scholarship taking in almost the whole world.

Lectures by many of the leading scholars already mentioned in this book were highlights, but so also were the more than twenty papers delivered by Africans as well as (mostly younger) scholars from China, Korea, Brazil, the Philippines, Australia, and New Zealand. For example, Chinese scholars, all of whom had been sponsored or befriended by Daniel Bays, presented carefully researched papers on how in the 1920s and 1930s groups of Chinese Christians began to develop indigenous forms of the faith as they selected from the offerings of Western missionaries what they felt was most helpful for their own setting. And there before our very eyes appeared a manifestation of what these scholars were describing. One of the key indigenous Chinese groups was the "Local" or "Lord's Recovery" Church associated with Watchman Nee. At Hammanskraal, members from the Pretoria "Local" Church, made up substantially of Afrikaners, attended part of our conference.

Other presentations on Christian developments in Ghana, Nigeria, Cameroon, Benin, East Africa, South Africa, Zimbabwe, Malawi, Korea, Nagaland, Mizoram, and Manipur offered instant access to what "the Christian world" had become. The opportunity to report on such matters for *Books & Culture* prompted me, better than any other stimulus could have done, to make at least a little sense out of this amazing cornucopia of information.

As this book's appendix indicates, with its checklist of things I have written on world Christian themes, it has been a privilege to explore such topics for a number of publications. Yet as it also reveals, *Books & Culture* came first.

❖

The notion that I should write books on world Christian subjects came up unexpectedly. Although I was certain that such interests would continue, I also knew that problems in American history and the challenges of intellectual life for evangelicals provided more than enough material for larger writing projects. Yet sometime around 2003 or 2004 a number of factors came together to divert me from what I thought was a settled course.

Andy LePeau, a senior editor at InterVarsity Press (IVP), was a longtime friend (and fellow committee member) at our church. Not coincidentally, he was also a helpful mediator with the United Kingdom's Inter-Varsity Press as he arranged for IVP-US to copublish my book, *The Rise of Evangelicalism: The Age of Edwards, Whitefield, and the Wesleys*, which appeared in 2003. This volume was the first of a five-volume series on evangelical Christianity in the English-speaking world that, as an outgrowth of earlier activities from the Institute for the Study of American Evangelicals, I was editing with my friend and fellow historian, David Bebbington of the University of Stirling in Scotland. After such expert help from Andy, I could not be offended by his friendly inquiry about "other books," though with several other long-gestating projects waiting in the queue, this temptation seemed easy to resist.

Yet when one of Andy's junior colleagues, Joel Scandrett, moved from encouraging words from afar to actual conversation over coffee in Wheaton's student center, things took a turn. I don't remember the exact date, and I'm not sure I can reconstruct the conversation exactly, but I believe it went something like this.

> Joel: You've been teaching courses in world Christianity and writing about such matters in *Books & Culture*. Don't you think you could do a book or books for us?
>
> Mark: No, there are too many other irons already in the fire.
>
> Joel: What if Carolyn could help?
>
> Mark: Hmmm.

Carolyn Nystrom, also a longtime friend from church, was at the time nearly finished with work for Wheaton's MA in theology, which she had pursued as a mature student. Her career as a writer, spanning several decades, had resulted in a number of Bible study guides, children's books, and other volumes aimed at church use. She had also worked successfully as a coauthor with others, most notably J. I. Packer. The query from Joel was probably prompted by his knowledge that Carolyn and I were well along in working together on a book that eventually appeared in 2005 as *Is the Reformation Over? An Evangelical Assessment of Contemporary Roman Catholicism*. She is also Joel's mother-in-law.

The suggestion that Carolyn might provide strategic help for writing books from my avocational interests came at the right time. Not long before, I had published *America's God: From Jonathan Edwards to Abraham Lincoln*, as well as the book from IVP. I thought (foolishly, as it turned out) that I was almost finished with a book long promised to Eerdmans that might say something positive about evangelical intellectual life. (This book, more or less a sequel to *The Scandal of the Evangelical Mind*, finally appeared in 2011 as *Jesus Christ and the Life of the Mind*.) Anticipating that I would end my teaching career at Wheaton, I was concerned about not simply hanging around until retirement. Most importantly, even piecemeal exposure to the altered circumstances of Christianity and the modern world had convinced me that the new Christian realities were important, should be studied, and deserved much fuller attention in traditionally Christian parts of the world like the United States.

The rest of the story gets more complicated. As explained in the next chapter, my career as a teacher was not going to end at Wheaton. For better or for worse, I was not going to simply glide into the sunset. But despite the hassles attending a move, multiplied new duties, and considerable carryover from earlier projects, Carolyn and I went ahead. Before long, we were also receiving a great deal of help from my wife, Maggie—first in her duties as a reference librarian at Wheaton and then as my part-time research assistant at Notre Dame. Even with that help, our manuscripts came in several *years* after the deadlines specified in the IVP contracts.

Carolyn's research helped materially in fleshing out the argument I wanted to make, and then illustrate, in a book that appeared from IVP in 2009, *The New Shape of World Christianity: How American Experience Reflects Global Faith*. The book's argument expanded on two of Andrew Walls's path-breaking essays. One had shown why the evangelization of North America was the great missionary story of the nineteenth century. The other had described how a voluntary and evangelical approach to Christian life, which reached its climax in American experience, had driven Protestant missionary efforts that spread throughout the world from the same nineteenth century.

My book expanded on Walls's insights by asking questions about the relation of Christianity in America to Christianity in the rest of the world. My suggestion was that although American missionaries had obviously exerted considerable influence, even more important was the way that Christian experience in much of the modern world replicated aspects of the free-form, voluntary, and bottom-up *style* of Christian faith that had developed in the United States after the American Revolution. This argument, which was illustrated through several case studies, allowed me to connect what I had long studied in American history with what I had more recently learned about the rest of the world. The book was dedicated to Andrew Walls, Don Church, and John Jauchen. It also included a memorial paragraph for Ogbu Kalu, who had died just before the book appeared; Ogbu was a Nigerian historian whose friendship and scholarship had touched me deeply.

The second book for IVP was an all-out team effort. Carolyn and I drafted biographical sketches for nineteen memorable modern Christians from Africa, India, Korea, and China. Maggie carried out a lot of research, took on the challenging task of securing permissions for illustrations, proofread the book, and constructed the index. Our goal was simple: to present accessible accounts of individuals who were important in modern Christian history but largely unknown in Europe or North America. Despite delays, competing demands, and a little confusion resulting from our move to South Bend, the effort proved unexpectedly satisfying. I had known something about figures like V. S. Azariah and Pandita Ramabai from India, William Wadé Harris and John Chilembwe from Africa, Sun Chu Kil from Korea, and Dora Yu and Wang Mingdao from China, but not much. Other figures like Mary Stone, one of the first female doctors in China, we discovered as we went along. The inclusion of Ignatius Cardinal Kung came about as I tried to explore more twentieth-century Catholic history for my teaching at Notre Dame. When IVP published *Clouds of Witnesses: Christian Voices from Africa and Asia* in 2011, all three of us were pleased with the result—not because the book was simple to write (it wasn't) and not because it made accessible biographical information that deserved much wider circulation (which it did). Instead, the writing process had been an unusually edifying experience as we tracked the high points and low points, the victories and the suffering, the cooperative achievements and the corrosive disputes, that marked the lives of a remarkable roster of notable Christian witnesses.

Books & Culture, IVP, and the other outlets with which I've been privileged to publish are themselves important mediators between conventional wisdom and the actual state of contemporary world Christianity. Without the opportunities they provided to explore with pen in hand, my life in the last nearly twenty years would have been a lot more relaxed. It would also have been intellectually and spiritually much poorer.

❖18❖

Notre Dame

In the summer of 2006, instead of continuing to ease toward retirement at Wheaton College, I encountered a fresh round of challenges by moving to the University of Notre Dame. Gratitude is still my prevailing emotion for the nearly three decades our family spent in Wheaton and for the privilege of working at the college. And ties continue to be strong with many friends and colleagues from those years. Yet the chance to teach at a research university, to work with graduate students who shared my interests in the religious dimensions of American history, and to once again follow George Marsden—this time in promoting graduate-level scholarship from a distinctly Christian angle—remain in my mind as compelling reasons for this late-in-life change of direction. With first-rate scholars like John McGreevy, Scott Appleby, and Kathleen Cummings, Notre Dame was continuing the key role in telling the story of American Catholicism that earlier generations (Philip Gleason, Jay Dolan, Marvin O'Connell, and others) had sustained so well for so long. When in 1994 Marsden joined our mutual friend Nathan Hatch on the history faculty, it meant that Notre Dame also became a premier center for studying Protestant aspects of the American past. George's "Macedonian (telephone) call" informing me that Notre Dame had opened a search for a senior

historian to carry on with his interests as he neared retirement precipitated my application.

Although questions about how I might contribute to teaching and
directing graduate students in American history was always the central
consideration for Notre Dame, world Christianity turned out to play
a complementary role. During discussions with the department, I
mentioned with some trepidation that I had much enjoyed creating a
course on the recent world history of Christianity and that, if possible,
I hoped to keep up *avocational* interests in the subject. The trepidation
came from knowing that as a research university, Notre Dame wanted
its faculty to work diligently on their *vocational* specialties—in my
case, American history. It came, therefore, as a pleasant surprise to
learn that the department would more than welcome such a course
since it had recently embarked on efforts to "internationalize the
curriculum." So it came about that this new academic setting made
it possible to continue what had become an important sidelight for
me as a historian and a Christian.

But how could such interests, which I had developed in an almost
completely Protestant environment, be adjusted for a setting where
most of the students who would take the class were Catholics? More
generally, I wondered if the Catholic ethos of Notre Dame would
affect my understanding of how and why the global dimensions of
Christian faith had become so pressingly important. I need not have
worried. Not only did the effort to explore Catholic dimensions of
recent world Christian history nicely complement what I had begun
to learn about Protestant phenomena, but a number of student and
faculty contacts also soon demonstrated that Catholicism—as both an
object of scholarly interest and a form of Christian faith itself—could
materially expand a Protestant's understanding of world Christianity.

❖

My cupboard was not entirely bare of Catholic content before
arriving at the new post. Several topics dealing with cross-cultural
concerns had long been a part of what I had tried to teach in general
church history courses. These included the world-historical significance of Boniface's eighth-century mission from the British Isles into

the heart of Europe, the pioneering ventures of thirteenth-century Franciscans into Islamic North Africa, and the notable Jesuit missions to the Far East that arose out of the Catholic Reformation of the sixteenth century. A long-ago reading of Shusaku Endo's novel, *Silence*, had left an indelible impression of the integrity of local believers and their Jesuit guides as they faced horrific pressure to renounce Christianity in seventeenth-century Japan. My interest in Canada had added some awareness of Jean de Brébeuf and his Jesuit companions as they carried out their pioneering mission to the Huron Indians in the early seventeenth century—and did so with what for that period amounted to considerable cultural sensitivity. The movies *Black Robe* and *The Mission*, and even more the reading that these films had sparked, provided some local color for Catholic efforts in Quebec and among the Guarani Indians of South America. With every other even half-awake observer of the recent past, I was also aware that the Second Vatican Council had altered Catholic relationships with almost every aspect of the modern world, developing regions and the West alike.

More to the point, I had become a regular reader of book catalogues—and some of the books—from Orbis Press, a publishing enterprise of the Maryknoll Fathers, the leading missionary order for American Catholics. While I did not know how Orbis managed to enlist its authors, it struck me forcibly that it was this American publisher, perhaps along with Eerdmans, that had done more than any other to explore the rapidly changing world situation. I knew that Orbis published a great deal of material on liberation theology, Latin America, and other expected Catholic subjects. But I was also greatly impressed that it had made a special effort to publish the Methodist Andrew Walls's two path-breaking books—and that it had also brought out significant books by Lamin Sanneh while he was still a Protestant, as well as other studies by first-rank Protestant scholars like Dana Robert, Samuel Hugh Moffett, Jehu Hanciles, Scott Sunquist, and Dale Irvin. Similar books by Catholics, including Sanneh after he moved to that communion, offered equal enlightenment. Simply observing the Orbis list over the years reinforced my sense that Catholic-Protestant cooperation was especially promising for realms beyond the Western world.

But there was still much to learn, and that learning came from many directions. Most direct have been the five opportunities, as of the 2013–14 academic year, to offer my undergraduate course. A feature of Notre Dame teaching that I had not experienced at Wheaton was the welcome presence of teaching assistants—PhD students who help organize the course, guide the weekly student discussions of assigned reading, handle much of the grading, and significantly broaden my own awareness as they bring their insights to the class. Thus, I learned about the worldwide spread (and multifaceted mission) of the Seventh-day Adventists from Nicholas Miller, about Korean American developments from Peter Choi, about life on the ground in China from David Komline, about important details of recent African history from Ben Wetzel, about complex processes of immigration from Philipp Gollner, and about how to write quizzes from Jeff Bain-Conkin. Graduate students have every right to expect direction from senior faculty, but I have also been delighted by what these unusually capable young scholar-teachers have taught me.

Notre Dame undergraduates have also been a source of much helpful instruction. From them I have been informed about the many American parishes where pastors or assistant priests hale from outside the United States. I have also learned something about the international Catholic networks that bring Latin American and Central European students to Notre Dame. From one student, who hesitatingly but accurately corrected what I was trying to say about Korean names for God, I heard the remarkable story of how a Catholic church in Moscow became the vehicle that brought a student from Korea to attend college in northern Indiana.

Fresh reading assignments for students have also meant expanded vistas for the instructor. They have made it possible to fit Joseph Kiwanuka, the first Catholic bishop in modern African history, into lectures I had earlier presented with only Protestant examples. Another assignment that left a permanent effect was Vincent Donovan's *Christianity Rediscovered*, an Orbis book that recounted the work of a Spiritan priest among the Masai in Tanzania. When Donovan became frustrated at the standard protocols with which he had been instructed, he set them aside and tried to communicate with the Masai as he saw the apostle Paul doing in the first-century Mediterranean world. The practical payoff is that I now usually include Donovan's "Masai Creed" in my syllabus as a first pointer to how the faith can be indigenized in new cultural settings:

> We believe in one High God, who out of love created the beautiful world and everything good in it. . . . We believe that God made good his promise by sending his Son, Jesus Christ, a man in the flesh, a Jew by tribe, born poor in a little village, who left his home and was always on safari doing good. . . . He was rejected by his people, tortured and nailed hands and feet to a cross, and died. He lay buried in the grave, but the hyenas did not touch him, and on the third day, he rose from the grave. . . .

In recent years John Allen's *The Future Church: How Ten Trends are Revolutionizing the Catholic Church* has served well as an assigned text. Its firsthand report on Catholic practices, difficulties, breakthroughs, and planning—from both the Vatican center and many far-flung places around the world—has offered not only a well-informed introduction to students but also much-appreciated illumination for the instructor.

Trying to expand lectures in order to include fuller attention to Catholic subjects has made it increasingly difficult to shoehorn everything into a semester-length course, but it has also led to deeper historical understanding. As an example, it has been rewarding to explain initiatives from various popes that promoted church revitalization in Latin America, responded to conflict in Communist China, and established procedures for monitoring the ever-expanding number of Catholic charismatics. That information has been intriguing in itself, but even more so when compared to corresponding efforts by various Protestants to deal with similar issues. It is an even more intriguing challenge to explore Catholic examples of evangelization, indigenization, European imperialism, decolonization, dialogue with world religions, internal disputes about social activism and/or eternal salvation, manifestations of the supernatural, and more. Trying to figure out why some of these Catholic experiences seem identical to what Protestant evangelicals now experience in many parts of the world, while others are so very different, provides the best kind of interpretive challenge.

❖

Not long after I came to the Notre Dame history department, the university's theology department initiated plans for a graduate program called "World Religions and World Church" (WRWC). This program combines attention to interfaith relations between Catholics and other religions along with study of the worldwide diffusion of Catholic and other forms of Christianity. Because of the interests that are explained in this book, I was drawn into this program as an adjunct faculty member. While other duties have limited my participation, it has been gratifying to take part at a distance. In the spring of 2009, as the WRWC program was taking shape, I much enjoyed the privilege of coteaching a graduate seminar with Professor Paul Kollman, a Holy Cross priest and distinguished missiologist who has published illuminating work on Catholicism in East Africa. The course was called "World Christianity: Historical and Theological Perspectives" and enrolled equal numbers of history students and theology students. Among its by-products, the class underscored what I had long sensed about differences in reasoning by historians and theologians. While interests certainly overlap, theologians tend to view historical contexts for how those contexts illuminate normative questions of truth, church order, and ethics. Historians tend to be concerned with how normative beliefs and practices take shape in specific or contrasting historical situations.

A more important benefit of this exercise in collaboration was instruction from the assigned readings and the stimulating class discussions that followed. From these readings and discussions, several memories remain fresh. First was the very high level debate between the anthropologists John and Jean Comaroff (whose books treat the history of Christianity in South Africa at great length) and the

historian of West Africa, J. D. Y. Peel (whose investigations into Anglican missionaries and African converts have been just as intense).
Where the Comaroffs are most impressed by how the imperial purposes
of colonizers shaped African Christians to their own purposes, Peel
responds directly by insisting that careful research shows that African
Christianity was always primarily a product of African agency. With
my prejudices leaning toward Peel, I thought his evidence was more
compelling than what the Comaroffs presented, but from both sides
the research was extraordinary, the arguments sophisticated, and the
interpretive conclusions challenging in the best way.

The course also served as my introduction to a series of books
from the University of California Press entitled "The Anthropology
of Christianity." This superb collection features ethnographic monographs describing Christian communities with the same objective empathy that members of this guild regularly exercised for non-Western
people but only recently have directed at—as it were—themselves.
The series includes books on Western communities as well as the
non-West. From it we read Matthew Engelke's *A Problem of Presence: Beyond Scripture in an African Church* (2005), an account of a
new Christian movement in Zimbabwe whose leaders say they do not
need the Bible because God speaks to them directly through the Holy
Spirit. Our discussion of the book was also empathetic, but from both
historians and theologians came penetrating questions about what
"Christian" means when the process of conceptual translation goes
on everywhere. Though I remain primarily a historian interested in
documenting changes over time, the sophistication of these anthropological studies gave me more opportunities for understanding the
diversity to be found in the contemporary Christian world.

Throughout the semester a consistent highlight was my fellow
teacher Paul Kollman. The class read his own account of the Catholic missions in Tanzania at the end of the nineteenth century that
both tolerated the enslavement of Africans and worked to convey the
benefits of Christian faith and Christian civilization to converts.[1] A

---

1. Paul Kollman, CSC, *The Evangelization of Slaves and Catholic Origins in East
Africa* (Maryknoll, NY: Orbis, 2005).

superb discussion followed on how in our own day—and with historical imagination, how in the late nineteenth century—to regard these
self-giving missionaries who yet did not scruple to take advantage of
human enslavement. Throughout the semester the whole class benefited from Father Paul's detailed knowledge of African history and
his encyclopedic grasp of the recent explosion of books and articles
on missiology and Christianity outside the Western world. Best of all
was his gracious spirit, which extended charity further than I could
manage for at least some of what we read about and some of the
authors who did the writing. For this class at least, I felt I could show
the same patient attention to students that he modeled, because the
students were so good.

❖

A telling moment in one of the class discussions allowed for deeper
reflection on what it means in the early twenty-first century for Catholics and evangelical Protestants to meet in the study of world Christianity. My years at Notre Dame have only confirmed the conclusions
that Carolyn Nystrom and I tried to explain in our evangelical assessment of contemporary Catholicism. If anything, my admiration has
grown for the clarity of classical Christian doctrine (on the Trinity,
Christ, the Holy Spirit, sin, the nature of the created world, Christian
ethics) that Catholicism maintains. The same must be said about the
lives of winsome holiness found in so many Catholic settings. Yet over
this same period my own commitment to the classical Protestantism
of the Reformation has also become stronger, especially accounts of
sin, grace, and salvation; the perspicuity of the scriptural message of
redemption in Christ; and the call to lay engagement that is so deeply
rooted in Protestant teaching (if not, sadly, in all Protestant practice).
Any deeper reflections on Catholic-Protestant matters moved in the
direction of seeing more clearly the genius of both evangelicalism and
Catholicism when they are functioning at their best.

The occasion was our discussion of Alvin Austin's *China's Millions: The China Inland Mission and Late Qing Society, 1832–1905*
(Eerdmans, 2007). This book provides a sprightly and well-researched
account of the mostly British missionaries of the China Inland Mission

and one of their most influential Chinese converts. Protestants in the class hardly blinked an eye when we read about Hudson Taylor's vision that led him to found the mission, about the middle and lower-middle class recruits whom Taylor sent to China without a whole lot of formal preparation, about the self-directed (often heroic, occasionally eccentric, sometimes very effective) activities of the missionaries, and about the relative lack of structure in the whole enterprise. Catholic members of the class were flabbergasted. How could anything securely Christian be so organizationally loose, educationally slight, and ecclesiastically casual?

From these contrasting reactions to the same book, I took away a stronger sense of how intrinsic the visibly organized church remains for all Catholic conceptions of Christian faith. By contrast, it also underscored how relatively unimportant questions of church order have been for most of the effective Protestant missions of the last two centuries and many of the Protestant-type Christian movements that have sprung up around the world. In our class discussions, it was noteworthy how much general agreement existed whenever the authority of Scripture or interpretations of any particular passage came up. Yet it was also clear that for Catholics biblical interpretation remained a carefully monitored collective task. Although we Protestants did not disparage the church's collective wisdom, we apprehended that wisdom informally instead of formally.

For me, the wide reading of the seminar, on top of a lifetime of reading on Christian subjects—and at least a modicum of personal experience—strengthened my conviction that the best expressions of the various Christian traditions draw very close to each other because each has drawn closer to Christ (some readers will recognize this formulation as stated with special clarity in C. S. Lewis's *Mere Christianity*). That same catalogue of reading has also strengthened my certainty that if for polemical purposes defenders of either Catholicism or Protestantism seek examples in the other camp of hypocrisy, malfeasance, tortured thinking, heretical teaching, and worse, they do not have a difficult task.

❖

My fondest hope about the experience of teaching at Notre Dame now for most of a decade is that the experience has made me a better historian as well as a better Christian. If this has not happened, the fault lies not with the new friends and colleagues I have made, but with myself.

❖ 19 ❖

The Story So Far

Enough has been said in the previous chapters to indicate what I think I have learned from becoming fascinated with the new shape of world Christianity. For someone who grew up in a missionary-minded household and who was brought to self-conscious adult faith by the Protestant Reformation, it cannot be a surprise that I would become captivated by the worldwide expansion of Christianity that has taken place over the last century. I hope the reasons for fascination and captivation have been communicated clearly enough.

Yet it is possible for fascination and captivation to sound suspiciously like unthinking triumphalism: see, where Christianity in 1900 was mostly limited to Europe, North America, and places colonized by the West, now it has spread nearly everywhere. Yes, of course, difficulties abound in the historical lands of Christendom, but just look at all the signs of vitality in so many new places. Doesn't the recent history of Christianity spell out the obvious: God's in his heaven, all's right with the world?

Not exactly. If our era has become the best of times, it remains also the worst of times. A religion anchored in the murder of God incarnate is a religion that takes the sinful proclivities of believers as

186

seriously as the entire world's need for redemption. If taking up the cross and following Christ is the pattern of holiness for individuals and communities, it is no less the pattern for the church universal. Consider the point in history we have reached. Age-old conventions that have linked persons, churches, and communities under the aegis of Christian faith—and more often for good than not—are unraveling in the West. The ever-expanding numbers who are turning to Christ in the Global South constitute the great marvel of recent history, but also pose real problems of continuity, discipline, endurance, impact, relationship, and maturity. The simultaneous spread of Islam in the very regions where Christianity has expanded so dramatically creates the potential for unprecedented breakthroughs in peaceful cooperation or all-too-familiar scenes of bloody conflict. In addition, if the newer Christian regions of the world lack some of the hypocrisy, colonial imperialism, racism, and materialism found in Western "Christian civilization," they also often lack that civilization's respect for the rule of law, its intermittently successful restraint of tribal violence, its commitment to peaceful democratic government in some form or other, and a great deal of the security it has provided for persons and property.

One helpful way of moving past mere wonderment toward sympathetic assessment of current realities and future possibilities is through case studies. Although individual cases do not have much predictive value, they remain the basis for all serious historical interpretation. They can also suggest the many-sided character of worldwide Christian expansion and push observers toward well-grounded, instead of romantic or superficial, assessments. To end this book, therefore, I am returning to the research that students have carried out in my classes, since that work has illuminated a much wider terrain than I could ever research myself. Their investigation of specific episodes, cruxes, problems, or breakthroughs suggests some of the realities that attend the dramatic recent spread of Christian faith throughout the world. Their research has moved not only in many directions geographically but also in many directions of evaluation—some studies revealing nearly ideal outcomes where the supernal promise of Christianity comes fully to life, others where the spread of the gospel has magnified distress, and many others where beatific and carnal results intermingle. As it happens, most of the examples that follow came from the work of Wheaton students, since the configuration of the Wheaton calendar allowed for more extensive research assignments than has been possible at Notre Dame.

This last chapter is not a conclusion; it is deliberately open-ended. Case studies can illustrate some of the generalities discussed in this book's earlier pages. But they also reveal the gnarled character of historical study itself—always revealing, almost never definitive. One of my strongest convictions has become that it is *always* too soon to pontificate. I hope that ending with these specific instances will steer readers away from that temptation, while at the same time sparking curiosity about specific situations in more-different places of the world.

Translation. The general picture outlined by Lamin Sanneh is almost everywhere confirmed: translating the Bible into new Christian regions bestows unusual dignity on those who speak the target language as well as conveying to them substantial control over the development of their faith. The textbook instance of that empowerment and control must be Korea.[1] When American missionaries and their early Korean converts chose the demotic variety of people's Korean, Hangul, for translating Scripture, the results were immediate and electric. In a context where Koreans had suffered from Chinese and Japanese imperial aggression—and consequent cultural abuse—the Bible in Hangul produced wonders. Christianity spread, literacy advanced, local empowerment developed, nationalism strengthened. Especially important were the colporteurs, most of whose names are lost, who mediated between publishers and the public. Much else has been significant in the lightning-quick emergence of Korea as a major force in world Christianity, but translation remains first in the rank of causes and effects.

1. Blake Killingsworth, "The Christian Bible as a Unifying Tool for Korean Nationalism from 1884–1919" (paper, Wheaton College, 2000).

Bible translation had an only slightly less dramatic impact in East Africa with the rendering of Scripture into Swahili.[2] Beginning in 1846, when a German missionary working for the Anglican Church Missionary Society published a Swahili New Testament, there has been a continuing turn to Christianity among the many who use this trade language for at least some regular purposes. But from early in the twentieth century, disputes among translators—usually without much consultation with Africans—produced two different versions of the Swahili Bible, one using Arabic-based terms, the other Bantu-derived words. Then in the 1970s came yet a third version, this one the work of East Africans themselves. Its thought-for-thought translation gained immediate popularity over the other two, which had followed the "formal correspondence" practice. The history of Swahili Bible translation, in simplest terms, is a success because of how the translation spurred church growth in the region. But it is also a complicated story of native versus foreign agency, competing translation theories, and occasional acrimony between sponsors of the different Bibles. In broadest perspective, translation appears everywhere not only as a foundational reality of Christianity as a global religion but also as a source of considerable turmoil.

Missionaries and locals. It is difficult to find a region of recent Christian development where missionary activity has not played a major part. Increasingly for careful observers, older stereotypes about crass imperialism or spiritual heroism are giving way to a much more nuanced picture. Especially welcome are the well-grounded works that for missionaries document many mixtures of self-giving altruism, cultural insensitivity, and sacrificial support for nationals. Careful research, in other words, yields deeper complexity.

In Taiwan, the West's opposition to Mao Zedong's Communist regime translated into strong missionary support for the Chinese Nationalists who were expelled when Mao triumphed.[3] That support, which was reinforced by widespread American publicity accorded

2. Carl Tullson, "Translation: God's Word, the World, and Human Agency" (paper, Wheaton College, 2004).

3. Trevor Powell, "Indigenization and the History of Christianity in Taiwan" (paper, Wheaton College, 2003).

the Christianity of Chiang Kai-shek and his wife, led to suppression of evidence documenting the Nationalists' despotic rule on the island, including at least one outrageous instance of mass murder. By contrast, during this same postwar period, some missionaries on the ground became the strongest supporters of the Taiwanese tribal people whom the Nationalists oppressed. The missionary record in Taiwan, therefore, shows that it makes a great deal of difference in considering which missionaries, when, and under what conditions.

India presents an even more complicated picture, and nowhere more complicated than in the Tirunelveli District of South India during the nineteenth century.[4] In the early years of that century, German missionaries broke with previous practice and attacked the caste system head on. Their criticism came not only as a great boon for lower caste Indians but also as a gratuitous offense to those in the upper castes, including Tamil leaders who had already emerged as the most distinguished Indian Christians of their generation. Questions about how Scripture should be translated entered into this story as well. The result, for someone paying attention to the details, was a picture of Christian expansion in which missionaries and Indians appear as both faithful followers of scriptural ethics and heavy-handed manipulators, as both those who have successfully adapted Christianity to local culture and those who prevent the faith from challenging local culture. The picture illustrates Andrew Walls's description of Christianity as an indigenizing pilgrim faith but also shows how much tension can exist between indigenizing and pilgrim principles.

Theology. Missiologists have expanded the Three Self formula that came from enlightened missionary statesmen of the nineteenth century by describing the need for a fourth "self." Self-support, self-government, and self-propagation were the standards that Henry Venn of the Church Missionary Society and Rufus Anderson of the American Board advanced as goals for mission service. Recent attention has fixed also on self-theologizing. In other words, a significant sign of maturity will be creative theological responses to the particular

---

4. Todd Melvin Thompson, "A Case Study on Christianity and Caste in Tirunelveli District, 1820–1830" (paper, Wheaton College, 2004).

problems confronted by new Christian communities. Not surprisingly, great interest—but also great controversy—accompanies efforts to carry out such self-theologizing.

In Latin America, liberation theology represented a major initiative of the postwar years. In Peru, unusually rancorous controversy developed over efforts at creating a theology from and for the great numbers in that country suffering in extreme want.[5] That controversy featured a clash of abstract nouns. From the Left: dependency, poverty, people, preferential option. From the Right: Marxism (as evil), property, control, tradition. Peru was also a setting where as conflict over liberation theology raged, in which Catholics took the prominent parts, some Pentecostal movements made striking advances without engaging in this debate. From the fine student paper that explored this local controversy, I took away an imperative to dig below the peaks of publicized controversy to explore the valleys where big words cash out (or not) in practice—and only then to assess how well the words mediate between Christian truths (the gospel narrative) and local realities (the human stories).

In East Africa, where Lutheran churches have grown rapidly over the last decades, a different theological challenge emerged.[6] Could traditional Lutheran formulas like "justification by faith" and "the priesthood of all believers" speak as powerfully in twenty-first-century Africa as they had in sixteenth-century Germany? This ongoing story witnesses a range of possibilities: repeat these classical formulations and look for the same personal transformations that occurred when they were first uttered; restate the formulas so that instead of focusing primarily on broken relations between God and individuals they apply to broken relations among humans (poverty, oppression, ignorance) that can be healed only by God; or try to fuse the personal relief that Lutherans have traditionally found in "justification by faith" with the relief from social injustice that remains such an imperative in the region. From the excellent student paper examining this situation, it

5. J. Peter Swarr, "Liberation Theology in the Modern Peruvian Church" (paper, Wheaton College, 2000).
6. Ann Cashner, "Lutheranism in Africa: Contextualizing the Faith" (paper, University of Notre Dame, 2008).

became clearer to me that self-theologizing is a necessity for newer Christian churches, but that as self-theologizing goes forward it can be very difficult for outsiders to evaluate. Wherever believers read Scripture, internalize the riches of Christian tradition, and respond to day-by-day living, God-honoring theology is sure to emerge—however long it takes for others to recognize what is going on.

Indigenization. The deepest impression I have carried from student research concerns the extraordinary variety entailed by the indigenization of Christian faith. In Western history, the record of indigenization has been just as varied and just as rich, but since that record has developed over more than a millennium, it seems less dramatic. In the proliferation of newer Christian regions the instances of indigenization have multiplied with both incredible rapidity and incredible diversity. The student work that has illustrated that rapidity and diversity underscores the incredible adaptability of this religion defined by the Word becoming flesh. The challenge from a human perspective is how to make some sense out of what can appear as simple confusion.

In trying to summarize work from my students, I am tempted simply to stand back in amazement—at, for example, the way that the YMCA in India maintained its evangelical character much longer than in the United States but also lost its Christian focus when it contributed positively to Indian nationalism.[7]

Or at the way that Christian attacks on caste have stimulated conversions from Hinduism to Christianity, but also from Christianity back to Hinduism.[8]

Or at how Christian missionaries flooding into the Soviet Union after the collapse of communism clashed among themselves and mostly failed to recognize the Orthodox deep structure that continued to shape Russian culture.[9]

7. Brandon Cole, "The Emergent Political Interests of the YMCA in India from 1875–1940" (paper, Wheaton College, 2006).

8. Daniel Hutchinson, "A History of Caste among the Christian Communities in India" (paper, Wheaton College, 2006).

9. Todd Okesson, "The Defensive Posture of the Russian Orthodox Church's Relationship with the State in Post-communist Russia" (paper, Wheaton College, 2000).

Or at how in China recently a Canadian Baptist pastor teaching at a major university was given free rein to teach the New Testament, while his supervisor, who was a member of the Communist Party, urged members of unregistered House Churches to become more sophisticated in their presentation of Christian theology.[10]

Or at how evangelical churches in Turkey have recently learned how to live within a strongly Muslim culture and still maintain an active public witness.[11]

Or at how in war-torn Kosovo, the United Nations took on some of the features that the ancient Roman Empire had assumed in the earliest decades of Christian history.[12]

Or at how believers among Australia's indigenous peoples can be caught between the empowering force of Christian faith and the long-standing positioning of Christianity as a driver of conventional Western culture.[13]

A huge range of such case studies now confronts the study of "world Christianity." Anchorage in the gospel story of One who came to seek and to save the lost, as well as awareness of successes and failures in past attempts at constructing "Christian civilization," give observers a place to stand. But the greatest challenge at this early stage of awareness about the rapidly changing world is to keep our eyes open.

❖

The new shape of world Christianity presents unusually sharp challenges for believers to live up to the high standards of their own faith. Lamin Sanneh has phrased one of these challenges pointedly: "The fact that disadvantaged peoples and their cultures are buoyed by new waves of conversion has created alignments of global scope at the margins of power and privilege. The paradigm nature of the

10. Grace Zhang, "A Sheer Wonder" (paper, Regent College, 2005).

11. Robert J. Wagner, "Christianity in Turkey: A Contemporary Portrait" (paper, Wheaton College, 2004).

12. Martha McComb, "The Role of the United Nations in World Evangelism: A Modern Day Roman Road" (paper, Wheaton College, 2002).

13. Kerry Schubert, "The Indigenization Process in the Development of Christianity amongst Traditional Custodians of Australia, Including a Case Study with a Wiradjuri Elder" (paper, Wheaton College, 2004).

realignment compels a fundamental stocktaking of Christianity's frontier awakening, and an imperative of partnership with it. When opportunity knocks the wise will build bridges while the timorous will build dams. It is a new day."[14] Other observers with experience in other corners of the opening Christian world are following Sanneh as they challenge believers to take seriously what the worldwide presence of the faith means for faithful Christian living.

Historians who attend to the developments prompting this book will be challenged both to affirm God's control over all human developments and to study energetically the visible causes and effects open to all other researchers.[15] The late Ogbu Kalu phrased this challenge as striving after "Clio in a Sacred Garb."[16] He meant that it is now necessary to observe rigorous historical methods as developed over centuries in the West ("Clio" is the muse of history) and at the same time acknowledge the manifest workings of God in time and space. While this challenge is daunting, trying to meet it has become more imperative than ever.

The end of this book is by no means the end of the story. Global Christian history is unfolding at a dizzying pace, with ever-multiplying questions about how the present has grown out of the past. A personal memoir must concentrate on friendships, schooling, students, local incidents, personal guides, and apparently haphazard connections. The full story, because of what it concerns, is infinitely larger.

14. Lamin Sanneh, *Disciples of All Nations: Pillars of World Christianity* (New York: Oxford University Press, 2008), 287.

15. Derek R. Keefe, "Some Challenges to Christian Historians in the West Posed by the Global Expansion of Christianity in the Twentieth Century" (paper, Wheaton College, 2006).

16. Ogbu U. Kalu, *Clio in a Sacred Garb: Essays on Christian Presence and African Responses, 1900–2000* (Trenton, NJ: African Research, 2008).

Appendix

Checklist of Publications on World Christian Themes

As an aid for writing the memoir, I was helped by compiling this list of my publications that deal with many of the themes, books, and authors that became grist for what has taken shape as a narrative. These publications are listed in chronological order, beginning in 1995.

"Midwives of the New South Africa" [on Alan Paton and Nelson Mandela]. *Books & Culture*, preview edition in *Christianity Today*, July 17, 1995, 33–34.

"Belfast: Tense with Peace." *Books & Culture*, November/December 1995, 12–14.

"In the Name of the Fathers: The Long Reach of Northern Ireland's History." *Books & Culture*, January/February 1996, 11–13.

"The Challenge of Contemporary Church History, the Dilemmas of Modern History, and Missiology to the Rescue." *Missiology* 24 (January 1996): 47–64. Revised as "The Potential of Missiology for the Crises of History." In *History and the Christian Historian*, edited by Ronald A. Wells, 106–23. Grand Rapids: Eerdmans, 1998.

"Translating Christianity" [on Andrew Walls, *The Missionary Movement in Christian History*]. *Books & Culture*, November/December 1996, 6–7, 35–37.

Review of Bruce Hoffman, *Inside Terrorism*. *Books & Culture*, November/December 1998, 15.

Review of Adrian Hastings, ed., *A World History of Christianity*. *International Bulletin of Missionary Research* 24, no. 1 (January 2000): 34–35.

"A Century in Books: Andrew F. Walls, *The Missionary Movement in Christian History*." *First Things*, March 2000, 55–56.

Review of F. W. Boal, et al., *Them and Us: Attitudinal Variations among Churchgoers in Belfast*. *Christianity Online*, June 25, 2000.

"Who Would Have Thought?" [concerning a South African conference on the recent spread of evangelical Christianity]. *Books & Culture*, November/December 2001, 21–22.

"Turning the World Upside Down" [review of Philip Jenkins, *The Next Christendom*]. *Books & Culture*, March/April 2002, 32–33.

Review of *World Christian Encyclopedia*, 2nd ed., by David Barrett, et al. *Church History* 71, no. 2 (June 2002): 448–54.

Review of Andrew Walls, *The Cross-Cultural Process in Christian History*. *Evangelical Missions Quarterly* 38 (October 2002): 516.

"Evangelical Identity, Power, and Culture in the 'Great' Nineteenth Century." In *Christianity Reborn: The Global Expansion of Evangelicalism in the Twentieth Century*, edited by Donald M. Lewis, 31–51. Grand Rapids: Eerdmans, 2004.

"The View of World-Wide Christianity from American Evangelical Magazines, 1900–2000." In *Making History for God: Essays on Evangelicalism, Revival and Mission In Honour of Stuart Piggin*, edited by Robert Dean Linder, 367–86. Sydney, Australia: Robert Menzies College, 2004.

Review of Andrew Porter, ed., *The Imperial Horizon of British Protestant Missions*, and two other books. *Books & Culture*, March/April 2004, 30.

"L'influence amèricaine sur le christianisme évangélique mondial au XXe siècle." In *Le Protestantisme Évangélique: Un Christianisme de Conversion*, edited by Sébastien Fath, 59–80. Turnhout, Belgium: Brepols, 2004.

Short review of J. D. Y. Peel, *Religious Encounters in the Making of the Yoruba*. *Christian Century*, October 19, 2004, 33.

Short review of Brian Stanley, ed., *Missions, Nationalism, and the End of Empire*. *Christian Century*, October 19, 2004, 33.

Short review of Hugh McLeod and Werner Urstorf, eds., *The Decline of Christendom in Western Europe*. *Christian Century*, October 19, 2004, 34.

Review of Chung-Shin Park, *Protestants and Politics in Korea*. *Journal of Religion* 85 (April 2005): 323–25.

Short review of Andrew Porter, *Religion versus Empire? British Protestant Missionaries and Overseas Expansion*. *Christian Century*, October 18, 2005, 23.

Short review of David Hempton, *Methodism: Empire of the Spirit*. *Christian Century*, October 18, 2005, 23.

Short review of Samuel Hugh Moffett, *A History of Christianity in Asia*, vol. 2, *1500–1900*. *Christian Century*, October 18, 2005, 24.

"What Has Been Distinctly American About American Presbyterians?" *Journal of Presbyterian History* 84 (Spring/Summer 2006): 6–11.

Short review of Ogbu Kalu, ed., *African Christianity: An African Story*. *Christian Century*, October 17, 2006, 23.

Short review of Jon Sensbach, *Rebecca's Revival: Creating Black Christianity in the Atlantic World*. *Christian Century*, October 17, 2006, 24.

"Looking South" [essay-review of four books on Latin American history]. *Journal of Religious History* 31, no. 2 (June 2007): 185–94.

"Nineteenth-Century Religion in World Context." *OAH Magazine of History*, July 2007, 51–56. Reprinted as "Nineteenth-Century Religion in World Context." In *America on the World Stage: A Global Approach to U.S. History*, edited by Gary W. Reichard and Ted Dickson, 55–71. Champaign: University of Illinois Press, 2008.

Short review of Liam Matthew Brockey, *Journey to the East: A Jesuit Mission to China, 1579–1724*. *Christian Century*, October 16, 2007, 35.

Short review of Alvyn Austin, *China's Millions: The China Inland Mission and Late Qing Society, 1832–1905*. *Christian Century*, October 16, 2007, 35.

Short review of Philip Jenkins, *God's Continent: Christianity, Islam, and Europe's Religious Crisis*. *Christian Century*, October 16, 2007, 35.

Short review of David Brion Davis, *Inhuman Bondage: The Rise and Fall of Slavery in the New World*. *Christian Century*, October 16, 2007, 35.

Review of Lamin Sanneh, *Disciples of All Nations: Pillars of World Christianity*. *Christian Century*, May 6, 2008, 38–40.

Review of Paul Freston, ed., *Evangelicals and Democracy in Latin America*; and T. O. Ranger, ed., *Evangelicals and Democracy in Africa*. *Christianity Today*, June 2008, 53–54.

Short review of Philip L. Wickeri, *Reconstructing Christianity in China: K. H. Ting and the Chinese Church*. *Christian Century*, October 21, 2008, 28.

Short review of Paul Freston, ed., *Evangelical Christianity and Democracy in Latin America*. *Christian Century*, October 21, 2008, 28.

Short review of Ogbu Kalu, *African Pentecostalism: An Introduction*. *Christian Century*, October 21, 2008, 28.

Short review of Robert Bruce Mullin, *A Short World History of Christianity*. *Christian Century*, October 21, 2008, 28.

Review of Philip Jenkins, *The Lost History of Christianity: The Thousand-Year Golden Age of the Church in the Middle East, Africa, and Asia—and How It Died*. *Books & Culture*, November/December 2008, 10.

The New Shape of World Christianity: How American Experience Reflects Global Faith. Downers Grove, IL: IVP Academic, 2009.

Review of W. R. Ward, *Early Evangelicalism: A Global Intellectual History, 1670–1789*. *Theologische Literaturzeitung* 134 (May 2009): 579–80.

"Does Global Christianity Equal American Christianity?" [Interview on *The New Shape of World Christianity*]. *Christianity Today*, July 2009, 38–40.

"Deep and Wide: How My Mind Has Changed." *Christian Century*, June 1, 2010, 30–34. Reprinted in *How My Mind Has Changed*, edited by David Heim, 53–64. Eugene, OR: Cascade, 2012.

Protestantism: A Very Short Introduction. Oxford: Oxford University Press, 2011. [Written as an attempt at a world history.]

Coauthor with Carolyn Nystrom. *Clouds of Witnesses: Christian Voices from Africa and Asia*. Downers Grove, IL: InterVarsity, 2011.

"Andrew F. Walls for Americans?" In *Understanding World Christianity: The Vision and Work of Andrew F. Walls*, edited by W. R. Burrows, M. R. Gornik, and J. A. McLean, 155–68. Maryknoll, NY: Orbis, 2011.

"What is 'American' about Christianity in the United States?" In *American Christianities: A History of Dominance and Diversity*, edited by

Catherine A. Brekus and W. Clark Gilpin, 382–95. Chapel Hill: University of North Carolina Press, 2011.

Review of Collum Brown and Michael Snape, eds., *Secularisation in the Christian World: Essays in Honor of Hugh McLeod. Church History* 80 (June 2011): 435–37.

Turning Points: Decisive Moments in the History of Christianity. 3rd ed. Grand Rapids: Baker Academic, 2012. [The last chapter, which is new for this edition, treats the 1974 Lausanne Congress on World Evangelization and the Second Vatican Council in terms of their worldwide impact.]

Review of David Hempton, *The Church in the Long Eighteenth Century*; and Dale Irvin and Scott Sunquist, *History of the World Christian Movement, Vol. 2: Modern Christianity from 1454–1800. Books & Culture*, November/December 2013, 9–11.

Index